THE SCIENCE AND CULTURE SERIES

Rev. Joseph Husslein, S.J., Editor

FATHER TIM

Father Tim Dempsey on the steps of the rectory with "some dirty, lovable imps of Sixth Street – God bless 'em."

HAROLD J. McAULIFFE, S.J.

FATHER TIM

THE BRUCE PUBLISHING COMPANY
MILWAUKEE

Imprimi potest: P. A. Brooks, S.J.
Nihil obstat: H. B. Ries, Censor librorum
Imprimatur: ✠ Moses E. Kiley, D.D., Archbishop of Milwaukee
April 24, 1944

(Second Printing – 1944)

This book is complete and unabridged and is reprinted in full accord with the rules and regulations of the War Production Board for the conservation of paper and other materials.

Printed in the United States of America

ACKNOWLEDGMENTS

The author is grateful to the publishers for permission to quote from the following works: *Recent History of the United States* by Frederick L. Paxson (Houghton Mifflin Co.); "Father Tim Dempsey's Biography" by Harry Winkeler (*The Mirror*); *A Saint in the Slave Trade* by Arnold Lunn (Sheed and Ward); *The Spirit of Catholicism* by Karl Adam, *Fire on the Earth* by Paul H. Furfey, *Mr. Blue* by Myles Connolly (Macmillan); *Christ in His Brethren* by Raoul Plus (Burns, Oates, Washbourne); *St. Francis of Assisi* by G. K. Chesterton (Doubleday, Doran and Co.); articles in *The Queen's Work; Safeguarding Mental Health* by R. C. McCarthy, *The Cheerful Ascetic* by J. J. Daly (Bruce); *Elizabeth Seton – An American Woman* by Leonard Feeney (America Press); *A Genealogical History of Irish Families* by John A. Rooney (O'Hart); verse in *Mission Fields at Home;* and articles in the *St. Louis Republic, Globe-Democrat, Star-Times,* and *Post-Dispatch.*

He is grateful, too, to all who have helped with this book by inspiration, suggestion, encouragement, criticism, information, and hard work of different kinds.

He wishes to dedicate *Father Tim* to his father and mother.

PREFACE BY THE GENERAL EDITOR

THERE is a wizardry about the life of Father Tim that casts enchantment on us all. At every turn the unexpected happens and the impossible apparently takes place. It is somewhat like sitting through the latest movie version of the Magic Carpet, but with facts instead of fiction on the screen.

But who was Father Tim?

He was the humble pastor of the poverty-ridden parish of St. Patrick's at St. Louis, dropped there in the midway of his mortal life by an inscrutable Providence. Around him, as he quickly found, lay a district frequented by hobo, thief, and gangster; infested with unsavory resorts and not lacking in haunts of vice, where even the police interfered but little.

Here, on the eddying tides of life, were whirled together the strays and discards of society, the helpless, the unfortunate, the flotsam and the jetsam of humanity. Who cared what became of them!

There were two ways open to Father Tim. One the safer, and apparently the saner, was the way of unaggressive parish duties, with due interment given to the latest murder victim. The other was the way of Paul of Tarsus, his heart eager with the folly of the Cross and aflame with zeal for the Crucified. The choice to be made was plain to Father Tim. There was a man's work before him and he would do it like a man. But the laughter did not die out of his eyes, and the smile did not fade on his lips, nor did the witty word fall less glibly from his tongue.

But out through the centuries was stretched to him the

sun-browned hand of the tent-weaver Paul, whose cry had sounded to him down the ages: "Rejoice in the Lord always; again I say, rejoice!" And it grasped in its own, with a manly grip, the great fighting hand of Father Tim.

It is not my purpose here to anticipate, except in a most general way, the true story of this book, or even to mention by name the numerous institutions established by Father Timothy Dempsey in the course of time. . . . One by one they rose, as if by magic, each at the proper moment, and together they answered the manifold human needs of his community – even to the purchase of a burial ground for the homeless wanderers.

Monumental in particular were his efforts to cope with the problem of the transients who in that day hiked and trudged their way to St. Louis as their terminal. He had, of course, his own free employment service which helped countless men to retain their self-respect or to overcome their *wanderlust*.

In a special manner Father Tim rose to epic greatness in the eyes of the people of St. Louis by his single-handed mastery of gangsterism, that for a time held the city locked in a reign of terror, lawlessness and murder, beyond the control of police. Giant in stature and a dynamo of human energy, Father Tim considered it his civic duty to throw himself into the struggle. In the same spirit, too, he undertook the difficult role of conciliator in labor disputes, and during an important period in the city's development was the unofficial conciliator of almost all the serious disagreements between men and their employers.

No wonder Father Tim became a national figure. Leaders in finance and in national politics, winners in sports and the prize ring, favorites of the stage and the screen, men from all walks and byways of life came to seek him out.

But most welcome always were the poor and most abandoned. If Father Tim did not make the Pauline mission voyages or follow to the ends of the earth in the footsteps of St. Francis Xavier, the Lord nevertheless destined for him his own unique foreign mission field. The fact is he had prepared for foreign mission work at St. Patrick's Foreign Missionary College in Carlow when the United States was still reckoned as a mission country, and so in coming to America had left home and native land to dedicate himself to the promotion of the Faith abroad. And if he did not go to the more remote mission fields, these instead came to him. At the door of Father Tim knocked the people of all tribes and tongues and nations, begging for lodging and food, asking for medical care or preservation from moral and physical ills, and withal he gave to them – as many as desired it – the food that gives strength unto life eternal.

One striking illustration may be mentioned here, the effort to meet a temporary problem in the depression years by his Free Lunch Room. Through this alone, at the date of his death some few years later, he had distributed in the proximity of 6,000,000 free meals to people of every creed and race and color, with no question asked of anyone, and no other slogan than: "Let no one go hungry!" No fewer than 13,000 free meals were distributed by him within one single day, and the total of free meals for the year beginning with September, 1932, was roundly about 2,500,000.

And what, then, were his secret funds?

Sure, and if anything could have aroused the mountainous merriment of big Father Tim it would have been to ask him that question: "Funds? God bless you." If ever there was a moneyless, penniless beggar, it was the same Father Tim, and in addition he had his debts to pay. But let the author describe this struggle. There were no government subsidies.

But Father Tim was not satisfied until he had added to his other perplexities his own monthly magazine, of which he was the editor. With that established, his bliss was supreme. He had a channel through which to promote his work and to propagate his ideas. Who knows in how many places his seed was to fall on good earth and to fructify, even beyond his own highest expectations? But of some such developments we do know, and they alone would have justified his labors.

We have here, then, the story of what one man could accomplish whose heart was filled with the true love of God, which necessarily implied love of the neighbor. Literally, it was the work of the Good Samaritan he was doing in a modern way.

But due credit, too, must be given to the author of this book. Intermittently for seven years he dedicated himself wholeheartedly to the task of following every clue that might yield him additional information. From endless items written by the newspapermen of Father Tim's day, who had faithfully followed his every step; and from the lips of persons of every class who, in whatever way, had come into intimate contact with Father Tim, the author gathered his material, carefully sifting the gold out of the sands.

Confidently, therefore, we hope that the result of his work, now made available to all, will prove a permanent inspiration to the Church in America, and that it will be of equal service to all outside the Fold, without distinction. For all alike have been appreciative of the great contributions made to humanity by Father Tim. And here once more comes back to us the truly Pauline trait of his labors, untiring and magnificently successful: "I became all things to all men, that I might save all."

JOSEPH HUSSLEIN, S.J., PH.D.
General Editor, Science and Culture Series
Saint Louis University.

CONTENTS

FOREWORD

I knew "Father Tim" for more than fifty years and with each of these succeeding years came increasing love and admiration.

He was singularly gifted by nature and grace, and while his chiefest role was that of miracle worker in the cause of charity, yet I can vision him as equally successful in many another vocation – for instance:

As an Irish chieftain of a thousand years ago leading his clansmen to victory or death – sheathed in armor I see him standing in his war chariot as he guides his foam-flecked steeds over the plains of Meath.

Or as in a century previous he stands in line to receive a cross and go forth a "Knight Crusader" to rescue the tomb of the Saviour from the hands of the Infidel.

Again I can vision him bowing his head as he receives the brown habit of a Brother of Saint Francis, later to share that same habit with the shivering beggar that stands outside the monastery walls.

Nor is it difficult to witness on the screen of a later century, an outraged and enslaved populace appealing to "Father Tim" to lead them out of the house of their bondage. Gladly he accepts from them the mantle of authority, and as a "Tribune" of old proceeds forthwith by voice and pen, and if necessary by sword, to restore them to their long lost heritage.

But our "Father Tim" chose to be a priest of God – and a priest he remained – a true priest he lived, serving the Lord in serving the poor, and a priest he died.

There are many proud names and high monuments in Calvary – there rest the founding fathers of our city – generals who led the nation's armies, governors of states, ambassadors of high rank, prelates whose fame will remain as long as the Father of Waters runs on to the sea — but great as any of these and more lovable is the kindly priest — the father of the poor — the friend of humanity — the beloved "Father Tim" who stanched many a tear, rebuilt many a human wreck, saved many a soul — and now lies resting with his fellow exiles beneath the great Celtic cross in Calvary.

I commend to our reading public the pages which follow. The book is elegantly written and carefully edited. Its perusal I am sure will elicit many a prayer for Father Tim and be an inspiration to his devoted successor to "carry on."

✠ JOHN J. GLENNON
Archbishop of Saint Louis

Chapter 1

FACING THE FACTS

MANY people in St. Louis knowingly shook their heads when Father Tim Dempsey threw open the doors of his Hotel for Workingmen in 1906. Wasn't the care of St. Patrick's church and school enough for the thirty-nine-year-old pastor? Wasn't it a bit revolutionary for a priest to venture from the sacristy and rectory and engage in such a mundane occupation as the management of a hotel? Hadn't the gandy dancers and "working stiffs" been getting along all right in the flop houses that dotted the lower end of town? What was this Irishman trying to do anyhow, reform the country?

Sure, America had been having its growing pains during the last quarter of a century. The scars left by a bitter Civil War were slow to heal. The southern gentleman still called his northern neighbor a "damned Yank," and the northerner reciprocated by hanging the sobriquet, "rebel," on his southern friend. The operation of liberalistic "laws" in economics had made big business lawless and too big for its own good and the general welfare. A few energetic and, for the most part, unscrupulous men had dominated the major industries. Many a strange bird had feathered his nest at the expense of the nation. The laboring man had been treated as something to be bought and sold like a piece of machinery with the result that the dignity of the human being had been overlooked.

Bloody struggles between labor and capital had convulsed the nation as the workingmen strove to better their condition in the face of a system that practised Darwin's doctrine of the survival of the fittest in the field of economic life. Marxian ideas of class struggle and hatred had seeped into American social thinking, manifesting themselves in syndicalism and socialism.

Against the thundering waves of liberalist opposition the American labor movement had been making slow progress. Adverse public opinion, caused by occasional acts of violence on the part of unbalanced zealots in the ranks of labor, had forced labor unions into secrecy during the seventies. But as the hope of individual independence declined because of the closing of the frontier and the disappearance of free lands, the unions emerged from their catacombs and began to evangelize on a national scale.

From the dust of the dead National Labor Union rose the Knights of Labor under Grand Master Workman Terence V. Powderly. Admitting all individual workers except lawyers, bankers, and saloon keepers, the Knights in the 1880's found themselves matching their lances against another federation established to preserve the autonomy of local union and at the same time to provide a national organization, namely, the American Federation of Labor, led by a vigorous London Jew of Dutch extraction, Samuel Gompers. The decline of the Knights after the Missouri Pacific strike in 1886 and the disappearance of the Henry George United Labor Party gave the new Federation a chance for rapid growth.

The panic of 1873 with its subsequent crushing depression was not without its effect on the workingmen. Strikes among the somewhat organized railroad workers and the disorganized miners tossed a wrench into the industrial machinery and jolted many previously complacent believers in *laissez faire* into wondering about the flawless operation of Adam Smith's "laws." The Chicago Haymarket riots in 1886 climaxed a series of strikes. Another disastrous panic and depression in 1893 stirred up and intensified labor unrest.

The previous year had already written the story of capital and labor in letters of blood as the Amalgamated Association of Iron and Steel Workers, in the Homestead plant of the Carnegie Steel Company, in vain demanded recognition by the company and protested against a reduction of wages for piecework. In 1894 the lowering of wages and the discharge of employees at the Pullman Palace Car Company near Chicago led to one of the worst strikes in American history. Supported by the American Railway Union under the fervent but somewhat erratic leadership of Eugene V. Debs, the strike ran its violent way for over a month until President Grover Cleveland sent in federal troops from Fort Sheridan. In the same year Jacob S. Coxey played the part of the pied piper in leading a peaceful march of the unemployed against the nation's capital, delightedly followed by a bevy of news-hunting reporters.

If industry during this quarter of a century had been trying to grow on the cone of an active volcano, agriculture had been maturing at least on a nest of busy ants. The decline in the value of silver, the general depressions in the 1870's and the 1890's, and the exorbitant hauling rates imposed by the railroads, all combined to make the lot of the farmer difficult. The very year of Tim Dempsey's birth in Cadamstown, Offaly County, Ireland, 1867, saw the formation in the United States of an agricultural benevolent society known as the Patrons of Husbandry, with a central organization called the National Grange. When the Granger movement and its successor, the Alliance movement, had finally managed to exterminate some of the most annoying ants, up sprang a dominantly agricultural party which came to be known as the "People's Party" or the "Populist Party." In the national convention at Omaha in 1892 the Populists complained that:

> Corruption dominates the ballot box, the legislature, the Congress, and touches even the ermine of the bench. The people are demoralized; most of the States have been compelled to isolate the voters at the polling places to prevent universal intimidation or bribery. The newspapers are largely subsidized or muzzled; public opinion silenced; business prostrated; our homes covered with mortgages; labor im-

poverished; and the land concentrating in the hands of the capitalists. The urban workmen are denied the right of organization for self-protection; imported pauperized labor beats down their wages; a hireling standing army, unrecognized by our laws, is established to shoot them down, and they are rapidly degenerating into European conditions. The fruits of the toil of millions are boldly stolen to build up colossal fortunes for a few, unprecedented in the history of mankind; and the possessors of these, in turn, despise the republic and endanger liberty. From the same prolific womb of governmental injustice we breed the two great classes of tramps and millionaires.

Bumper crops and rising prices coupled with disunion among Populist leaders melted this temporary accumulation of the discontented into nothingness during the next few years and made the platform of 1892 sound even to Populist ears as so much bombast.

Influenced by discontented labor leaders, the Populist Party had complained that imported pauperized labor beat down wages of urban workmen. There was no denying the temporary bad effects of the influx of European immigrants on the wage scale. The body politic suffered indigestion in trying to assimilate the millions of Europeans who cast themselves on American shores in the hope of enjoying peace and fair treatment. A degrading system of absentee landlordism and continued poverty and suffering had wrenched enough Irishmen from their homeland to affect the balance of political parties. For the most part the Irish immigrants cut the roots that bound them to the soil and settled down to a new way of life in the cities. German and Scandinavian immigrants put their strong hands to the ax and the plow. As the migration from northern Europe began to decline around 1900, the migration from southern Europe grew. The southern elements tended to remain isolated in racial groups, maintaining as far as possible their native languages, customs, and habits.

As immigration mounted and as industry and transportation expanded, cities assumed a new importance in American life. In twenty years, from 1870 to 1890, the number of cities with fifty thousand population rose from twenty-five to fifty-eight. Rapid urbanization brought a train of problems to tax the ingenuity of social thinkers and religious workers. The numerous poor were forced to bury their respectability and individuality in crowded ugly tenements and struggle along from day to day on wages that wouldn't support the house dog nowadays. The pressing needs of communities demanded the formation of water, gas, and electric companies, and the establishment of transportation facilities. As in our own day, dollar-hunting city officials were willing to betray their sacred trust and the best interests of the people in meeting these fundamental needs.

Saloons, gambling dens, and brothels provided unwholesome diversion for those who had the money to spend and the time to waste. The ministers of religion found themselves handicapped in their salutary work because of shortage of funds and personnel and because of language difficulties and noncooperation. If socialist thought achieved nothing else of real value, it at least broke down to some extent the liberalist, "dog-eat-dog," rugged individualist view of human society. Numerous noble-minded people became aware of the fact that there was a social problem and began to investigate how the other half lived. Their findings shocked Lilian D. Wald into opening the Henry Street Settlement in New York. Jane Addams established the Hull House in Chicago, and a host of settlements sprang up in various other cities, some under religious, others under secular auspices.

The idea of social responsibility, so long stressed by Pope Leo XIII, was beginning to penetrate a society whose moral sense had been dulled by the popularization of false principles set up in the sixteenth and subsequent centuries. Victory over Spain in the war of 1898 awakened the United States to a sense of world responsibility.

All these happenings had their repercussions in the old Mississippi river city, founded in 1764 by Pierre Laclede and Auguste Chouteau and placed under the protection of the beloved King of France, St. Louis IX. Originally French, the city had become by 1900 the melting pot of nationalities, with German and Irish predominant. Colonization societies had succeeded in persuading thousands of immigrants to push westward from the Atlantic coast and settle in the more spacious Midwest. The handy location of St. Louis on railroad and steamship lines had invited steady settlement.

Attracted by the availability of raw materials, power, and transportation, numerous possessors of capital had launched the city on its impressive industrial career. Like bees around the hive, workers moved in and out of shops and factories, except during those periods of dislocated economy when they were forced into unwilling idleness. The same conditions that invited struggle between capital and labor in other parts of the country prevailed in St. Louis. Religious zeal and humanitarian sentiment had tried to keep up with the growing educational and charitable needs. Enterprising citizens endeavored to maintain the cultural tradition of the city by encouraging the best in music, drama, and the other fine arts.

In the lower north-central part of town lay St. Patrick's parish. Built in the 1840's principally for the English-speaking Catholics, the red brick church on the northwest corner of Sixth and Biddle had long been the center of vigorous Irish parochial life. But by the time a young Irish priest named Tim Dempsey assumed the burdens of pastor in 1898, the parish was very much on the decline. Whole blocks of homes had been razed to make room for the railroad yards and factories. Fashionable homes were converted into rooming houses. The inevitable brothels and dives had given the district an unsavory reputation. Instead of embracing 20,000 souls as it had during the 1870's, the parish could claim only a few thousand permanent residents, many of whom were not English speaking.

At a time when newspaper stories rumored the probable sale of the church, school, and parochial residence and the establishment of a new St. Patrick's in another part of the city, a friend greeted the young pastor with the remark, "Well, Father, I see they are going to sell the old church at last, but I suppose you will stick to the ship until it sinks." Father Tim smiled and remarked in an offhand way that disguised his inner determination, "Maybe I will be able to keep the ship from sinking."

Tim Dempsey had no megalomaniac ideas about reforming the country, or the city, or even the parish. His youthful idealism did not keep him from walking with his feet on the ground. Since his arrival in America, in 1891, fresh from ordination at the famous foreign missionary college of St. Patrick in Carlow, he had served a pastoral apprenticeship in various parts of the St. Louis archdiocese. He had learned to grapple with problems as they exist. He was not the type to run around an obstacle; he would look at it, study it, then remove it, or jump over it.

He looked at the parish. It wasn't a normal parish. The majority of the residents spoke Slavic, Hungarian, Hebrew, or Italian. People were coming and going with a rapidity that defied any accurate account of parishioners. Enough Irish remained to remind one that St. Patrick's had been an Irish parish and enough returned on each St. Patrick's day to make one think that it was still the glory of the Irish. Colored people were moving into the district. The people were as poor as any of Dickens' unfortunates. It was the sort of place that refined ladies would visit when they wanted to go slumming for a thrill. Fists flew on the least provocation, and guns and blackjacks were as common here as penknives in more refined quarters. Window tappers invited to sexual license and the swinging doors of saloons often opened on brawls, high gambling stakes, and drunkenness. The ten commandments took a beating, and Father Tim knew it.

But he also knew that under the surface badness was a substratum of fundamental goodness. He would work on that. If the tough environment shocked his tender sensibilities, he could swallow his repugnance with the help of God. After all, he was a missionary and here were souls to be saved.

The problem of the itinerant workman especially worried him. Hundreds of railroad day laborers and farm workers "floated" into the big river town when the first cold breezes began to make their teeth chatter and out again when they could throw away their winter underwear. The majority gravitated into the slum district where St. Patrick's dominated the sky line. The farm workers, the "Oakies" of that day, were known as "working stiffs," and would, in the words of Harry Winkeler, "follow the sun like a swarm of constructive grasshoppers, helping to plant and harvest and moving along until they arrived in the wheat fields of the northwest. With the harvest days over and the chill winds blowing strong across the plains, these workers would hop the freight trains for the big cities. In the long trek homeward they were preyed upon by holdup men, sheriffs, and other unspeakable gleaners of the unfortunate. If they were lucky enough to arrive in the big city with some cash left, they would go to some flophouse and pay a few months' rent in advance. The barrel houses, the prostitutes, and the hangers-on of the bawdyhouses and cheap dives would get what was left. This meant that for the rest of the winter there would be an epidemic of beggars, holdups, and soup kitchens. . . . It was upon these oppressed and exploited victims of fate that radicalism fattened. The I.W.W. became the patron of many of them, and 'Big Bill' Haywood, with his 'one big union' thesis, was their messiah."

The young pastor could have let these men go their way; he could have excused himself by reflecting that the permanent residents gave him enough work; he could have been a "sanctuary" priest choked by complacency and mediocrity. But no, he was a man of action. Something had to be done for these men and he had to do it. Whether a man was a Catholic or not, he should enjoy an environment as free as possible from the occasions of sin and conducive to the practice of virtue. That's why Father Tim Dempsey opened St. Patrick's Hotel for Workingmen in 1906. Let people think him crazy; he felt that he was doing the right thing and that's all that mattered.

Chapter 2

FOR MEN WHO WANTED TO BE DECENT

FATHER TIM knew that he was right when he conceived his new idea of a workingmen's hotel. In routine administration of the last Sacraments he had sufficient experience to bring home with sledge-hammer effect the correctness of his plan. He had brought Holy Communion to dying men in disreputable lodginghouses where the bunks were so close together that he could scarcely get in between them. He had seen those "coops" or "cages," a bit of space surrounded by sturdy wire, where a tired man might woo slumber with a fair amount of security that his personal belongings wouldn't disappear during the night. He had seen flophouses that specialized in "hot-beds," so called because the beds were used in shifts for twenty-four hours. He knew, too, how callous the majority of lodginghouse keepers were.

He couldn't erase from his mind a visit he paid to an old peddler who made a slim living selling shoestrings, collar buttons, needles, and thread. Cooped in a "room" that was more like a doghouse, the old man was dying, helpless and friendless. Thinking that the operator of the rooming house had an ordinary dose of the milk of human kindness, Father Tim suggested that the friendless peddler be taken to a hospital. The operator swept steely eyes over the athletic figure in clerical black, then barked in words coated with anticlerical ice, "Why don't you send him there? – but I guess you people won't do anything without money."

Father Tim felt as if he had been knifed. He took the imaginary knife, liquefied it over his very real temper, and then gave the insolent clerk a warm piece of his mind. He rushed to the nearest livery stable, drove the carriage to the lodginghouse, carried the old man down the stairs himself, and brought him to St. Mary's Hospital where, he knew, "God's noblest daughters, the hospital sisters," would take care of him until death. How could a man live decently in such surroundings as that rooming house provided, reflected Father Tim, and how could he die decently?

If the lodginghouse didn't ruin a man, the saloons would. Tim Dempsey knew the power of drink. As a young man he had to fight many a personal battle for control over the "spirits" that were in bottles.* He had seen enough lives wrecked on the rocks of excessive indulgence to frighten himself into temperance and to make him an apostle among indiscreet drinkers. Two experiences early in his pastorate convinced him of the degrading influence of the cheap saloon on the characters of the men in the neighborhood of St. Patrick's.

As he was passing by a cheap saloon one day, a policeman with a worried look on his face emerged. "Father, there's a man dying in there." Father Tim crashed through the swinging door. The bartender, a bit bewildered and at the same time on guard against a rough house, whipped out a revolver. When he recognized the pastor, he hid the revolver and kept on supplying the orders of his customers. Business was business. What did it matter that a man was dying or dead? He motioned Father Tim to a back room. The man was dead. Four stupidly drunk friends were sitting around the dead body and drinking from the beer can, totally oblivious of the death of the man. It was almost enough to sicken Father Tim's stomach.

Another sickening experience happened on one Christmas morning. The doorbell of the rectory rang. Two poorly clad

---

*This statement, based on reliable testimony, has been contradicted by some of Father Tim's friends.

men stood at the door. They urged Father Dempsey to hurry to a certain saloon where a man was close to death. The three of them hurried to the place. When they asked the bartender just where the dying man was, he looked stupidly at them through bloodshot eyes and slumped back in a chair, dead-drunk. They rushed to a room at the back of the bar. There was the dying man, stretched out on a chair tilted against the wall. The air was thick with the smell of whiskey, cigar smoke, and dirty clothes. Father Tim looked pityingly on the poor man and felt his pulse. The fellow seemed almost lifeless. His legs and feet had swollen so much that his shoestrings had broken. His unkempt face seemed corpselike under the play of the gas light. Father Tim took out the oils, administered conditional Extreme Unction, and called for an ambulance. The hapless derelict died on the way to the hospital.

The whole wretched situation offended Father Tim's sense of justice. He likened the majority of rooming-house operators and saloon keepers to vultures waiting to pounce on their prey. Taking advantage of human weakness, they were draining men's pockets and corrupting men's souls. There was no use telling the men to brace up, find a decent boarding-house, and live like decent men. They would shrug their shoulders and with a simple unanswerable question demolish the force of the exhortation. "Where will we go, Father?" they would say. "These are the only places that give us a shelter; we meet our friends here, boys off the trail like ourselves; we have no home and misery loves company."

That simple question, "Where will we go, Father?" had to be answered. The answer was to provide a decent home for men who wanted to be decent.

But this was easier said than done. Father Tim was a poor pastor in a very poor parish. He had enough experience with management to know that a home for men couldn't be run on mere good will. He would have to rustle up some money. Archbishop Glennon's approbation would have to be secured.

He would have to scout for a site. Should he rent an old place or build a home? These and other problems racked the young pastor's brain. His impetuous nature chafed at the necessity of solving one problem after the other. Fortunately he had made friends among the wealthy as among the poor. Many of these wealthy friends were sympathetic to the idea of opening a hotel for workingmen. Knowing the character of Father Dempsey, they were willing to donate money for the project. Others laughed at the whole idea. What did this young Dempsey think he was anyhow, the redeemer of the unredeemable? Let these off-scourings of humanity rot or commit suicide; good riddance of bad rubbish, said they.

On St. Patrick's day in 1906 the Archbishop promised his hearty support to Father Tim's plan. After a great deal of investigating, Father Tim found the building he wanted, a three-story brick affair on the northwest corner of Eighth and Franklin, not far from some of the worst lodginghouses and saloons in the city. He would put the hotel where the wanderers couldn't miss it.

A letter from the Archbishop in November, 1906, encouraged him.

My dear Father Dempsey:

I was very much pleased to hear that you are about to form a workingman's club with a rooming house combined. I feel sure that it will be a great success from the start as it will also be an evident blessing.

The late venerable Pontiff, Leo XIII, urged repeatedly the formation of Catholic Workingmen's Unions. You may not be able to achieve all he wished, but you will at least minimize the evils which beset the laboring man, and save him from those places where his faith, morals, and manhood are being undermined and destroyed.

Unfortunately just at present these latter places appear to be the only ones in our large cities that offer to the workingman even the semblance of a welcome. Their bright lights allure him, then their bad drinks destroy his body, and the miserable associations ruin his soul.

I have before my mind the hard-working Irish laboring man who all through the fine weather works and saves some money, then gravitates towards the "resort," and in a few days all his money is gone and with it his so-called friends and patrons.

If you can form somehow a combination club and boardinghouse where our laboring men can obtain at a very moderate price a clean bed, comfortable surroundings, with a well-lighted and decently equipped club room, you will find many willing to help you in the good work.

Sincerely yours,

✠ JOHN J. GLENNON, Archbishop

Mention of the Irish laboring man stirred a sentimental strain in Father Dempsey. Yes, it was true; a great number of these workmen were Irish. They were exiles from his homeland. Why not call the hotel, then, "The Exiles' Rest"? Yes, even though many of the guests might not be Irish, he would call the hotel "The Exiles' Rest." There was a poetic touch about the name that could make one forget the sordid environment of Franklin Street. In December the renovated building was ready for occupancy. Father Tim's heart lagged as he thought of the formal opening. Would the men respond to his efforts? Would his invited guests approve of the way he had spent their money? Would the wiseacres who referred to the projected hotel as "Dempseys' flophouse" soon be rejoicing over the house that flopped? Tim tried to dismiss his worries with the thought that God would take care.

The big day came. The Archbishop, other clergymen, Mayor Rolla Wells, Judge O'Neill Ryan, John S. Leahy, Festus J. Wade, William J. Kinsella, and various prominent St. Louisans were the first to write their names in the hotel register. Before night fell, fifty-three homeless men had taken all the available beds. Father Tim had shaken the hand of every single one of them and made them feel that they were doing him a favor by coming to his hotel. No impersonal service of his fellow man for him. He loved each man as an individual human being. He was not concerned about their past. His men would not be "cases"; they would be Joe, Pat, Jack, Pete, and Bill. As he went to bed that night, he realized that he had committed himself to a nerve-trying, arduous job, but he was glad. God would take care.

In a short time it was evident that the Franklin Street building was inadequate. Father Tim's faith in the fundamental goodness of human nature had been confirmed. Hundreds of men showed that they wanted to be respectable by seeking to get into this "decent home for men who wanted to be decent."

It was now that Father Tim looked longingly at the big school building on Seventh Street which had been constructed in the 1870's to serve the children of St. Patrick's. Its excessive cost, together with the panic of 1873, had caused hundreds, if not thousands, of families to move out of the parish. Finally the Public School Board had bought it at a low price and re-named it Shield's School. Now it was vacant. With the help of Harry Hawes and Mayor Rolla Wells, Father Tim's proposition of leasing the old school as a hotel was unanimously accepted by the Board, and in December, 1907, the hotel opened for business with accommodations for four-hundred men. In quick succession the name changed from "The Exiles' Rest" to "St. Patrick's Hotel for Workingmen" and finally "Father Dempsey's Hotel for Workingmen." Popular demand forced Father Tim to retain the latter name.

A short time after the formal opening he called to see Jack Ryan, a first-class humorist of remarkable mimetic powers who was clerk at the pretentious Southern Hotel where only the wealthy and socially prominent stopped. After the usual greetings he asked about the state of business. Ryan answered that it was a bit slow. With mock solicitude Father Tim sympathized, "Jack, my boy, I hope we're not hurting you any."

As a matter of fact, Father Dempsey's Hotel for Workingmen was hurting nobody but the operators of saloons, rooming houses, and brothels. It offered the guests "clean, comfortable beds with comfort and linen, hot and cold baths, shower or plunge, shoe blacking and brushes, comb and brush, access to all the leading newspapers and magazines, towels and soap, ventilated locker and key, piano and music in recreation room, stationery, employment thro' free labor agency, safe in the office for valuables, telephone service." And all this for ten cents a day, until the time of the first World War when the price had to be boosted to fifteen.

For men used to sleeping in flophouse "cages" and "hot-beds" – where night visitors of the insect variety feasted, where the air stank from dirty linens, smelly bodies, and liquor, and where one enjoyed about as much privacy as the old-time French kings who were born, lived, and died in public – clean, comfortable beds with fresh linen were a luxury. Father Tim realized, too, that a bath and change of clothes could do wonders in restoring a broken man's self-respect. He was not so foolish as to believe that a wholesome environment would absolutely eliminate sin and crime, but he properly estimated its value in removing the occasions of sin. His hotel restaurant advertized:

> Meals for a nickel, a dime and fifteen cents. Genial clerks, cooks and waiters, ready to cater to the keenest appetite and the most slender purse. Everything clean and neat. We buy the best meats, vegetables, coffee, bread, milk, and cream. We pay our employees good wages, thus insuring perfect satisfaction to our patrons. When you are down-town and fatigued after business, try a cup of our excellent coffee.

Even though the charges for hotel facilities and meals were so ridiculously cheap, many men couldn't afford to pay. Should they be turned away? Father Tim's policy was to let them write the charges on the cuff – if they had a cuff. When times got better, they'd pay what they owed. But if and when times didn't get better for these particular men, he found himself providing many free lodgings and free meals. He had no intention of making the hotel a charity institution, however. It was better, he judged, to maintain a small charge in order to safeguard the proper pride and independence of his guests.

His hotel was intended for "men of the road" who were of the working class type that travels from center to center of business activity or labor opportunity for the purpose of securing work, and not for the "men of the road" who were of the loafing type, the professional tramp or hobo or bum, who travels from place to place in order to get away from work. But if a man was "flat broke" and really needed help, and there was room at the hotel, that man found a place there. There were below-zero nights when one could not walk down the halls of the hotel without stepping on the unprotected chest or leg or arm of a sleeping man because so many had been allowed to get a free night's sleep on the floor after all the beds were taken. During the bitterly cold month of December, 1907, a total of 4428 men slept on the floor.

Many of the guests were rovers by disposition. They wouldn't stay in one place and at one job for a long time. But others were rovers by necessity. They had to go where the work was. For these men Father Dempsey began to find steady employment in St. Louis. His prospectus advertized, "We supply all kinds of labor and help. . . . You may have a preference for a man of a certain nationality. We have Indians, Americans, Irish, Scotch, English, German, Polish, Rumanian, Italian, Bohemian, Slovanian, Spanish, Norwegian, Danish, French, Belgian, Swedish, Dutch, Greek, etc."

Father Tim was a one-man free Labor Agency or Employment Bureau. He forced a number of crooked agencies out of existence. Business firms and families called Father Tim when they needed workers. A lady would phone and say, "Father, I need a yard-man." He would reply, "I know just the man you want, ma'am." Or someone would ask for a housemaid. He knew just the girl for the job. Some girl in the parish would be thanking him for an opportunity to earn a bit of money.

Father Tim's guests or "b'ys," as he called them, were of a wide variety of religions, nationalities, occupations, abilities, interests, and ages. Jack Ryan of the Southern Hotel snared the spirit of the hotel in a bit of verse that became famous among Father Dempsey's friends.

A wand'ring minstrel tarried here,
Where sounded discord's knell,
And men as equals meet and part
At Father Tim's Hotel.

And pointing to the many groups
That strangest fates befell,
'Twas thus he ravelled off his tale
In Father Tim's Hotel:

"One fought for that old Southern cause,
Loud rang his rebel yell;
He's chumming with a Yankee now
At Father Tim's Hotel.

"The Russian Cossack rests in peace
As sound as a new bell,
Though he sleeps beside a sturdy Pole
At Father Tim's Hotel.

"The Frenchman sighs for lost Alsace,
His dreams no tongue can tell;
He wakes to greet his German foe
At Father Tim's Hotel.

"And Doctor Elliot, Harvard's chief,
Might change his views on hell,
If he tackled Michael Gallagher
At Father Tim's Hotel.

"Just watch that roaring A.P.A.
As he hears St. Patrick's bell,
He's cheering for the Pope of Rome
At Father Tim's Hotel.

"But there's the strangest sight of all,
Pat Ryan, of old Clonmell,
He tolerates an English lord
At Father Tim's Hotel."

God's blessings on those exiles
Who in peace and union dwell
Beneath the hospitable roof
At Father Tim's Hotel.

Then, success to Father Dempsey
And Father Dunne as well,
The founders of the Newsboys' Home
And the Workingmen's Hotel.

There were good men and bad men, but, as Father Tim put it, "The bad men did not stay long." He was able to boast that there never "was a fight in the house." Perhaps the main reason why there never was a fight was that they were afraid of what "the big fellow," as they referred to him, might do. When he threatened offenders with a good beating, correction or amendment usually followed. Drunkenness was the big enemy. His understanding and tolerance of drinking men was immense. To the natural schemes of the present day as Alcoholics Anonymous, he added supernatural methods of curbing the vice. In the evening he might call up the hotel and ask, "Is Jim in?" Then, "Is he full?" Depending upon the answer, he would say, "The villain – after all I said to him," or "That's fine," and turning from the phone, he might remark, "Jim hasn't taken a drop in weeks. It's wonderful."

Father Dempsey made a practice of learning the names of all the men he met and worked with. His was a personal concern about every last one of the human beings who came into his life. They were not "cases" to be analyzed, summarized, card catalogued, and then treated in a machinelike way, nor were they merely economic factors. His personal interest showed itself in the fact that he always answered the doorbell and telephone himself when he was in his prime. In his two or three daily visits to the hotel he would look at the register for new names and become acquainted with the newcomers. He did not inquire into their past lives. He won their hearts; then, if they wanted to talk, all right; he would be a willing listener. They liked that.

On one of his regular evening visits he put the usual question to the night clerk, "Do any of the men want to see me about registering?" The clerk replied, "Yes, Father, there are five looking for you. Their names are Harrigan, Riordan, McGovern, McCormick, and O'Connell."

"Pray for us," said a voice from the shadows in the hallway.

Father Tim turned in time to see a little old man reverently lifting his cap as the last word came from his lips.

"What do you mean, my man?"

"I thought, Father," said the little old man apologetically, "he was recitin' the litany of the Saints."

The humor of the situation was not wasted on Father Tim who had a habit of looking for the humorous things of life. This habit together with the habit of looking for the good that's in other people kept him balanced. He realized that

> There is so much bad in the best of us
> And so much good in the worst of us
> That it hardly behooves any of us
> To talk about the rest of us.

Whenever he could say something good about a person, he seized the chance.

After running the hotel for two years, he had something good to say about his men: "We never had the slightest fear but that the 'men of the road' were amenable to good influence, that they were not different from other human beings, that they realized deep down in their hearts that men were not born to roam without any fixed place of abode. We knew that kindness would not be wasted, or at any rate it would not hurt the giver, that a kind word never broke a tooth, and that many a time a man's tongue broke his nose; and now after two years of experience with 15,000 to 20,000 men, we never shook the hand of a 'man of the road' that we don't want to meet again. . . . If there are mean men on the road, either they did not visit our hostelry or they forgot their failings during their stay with us. The guests of some of our pretentious hotels might well pay a visit with profit to 1111–1121 North Seventh Street where one cannot help noticing the absence of all vulgarity either in word or act, the eagerness of each one to contribute to the happiness of his fellow, the respect invariably shown to visitors, the effort made by all to show appreciation for what has been done for them."

Interest in Father Dempsey's Hotel for Workingmen grew as individuals and the newspapers related stories of the good that was being done. Inquiries about the work flooded Father Tim's office. Even with the help of his efficient, one-legged clerk, William McDonald, Father Tim who was an inveterate letter-writer shouldn't keep up with the flood of mail. What to do, what to do? His friend Father Dunne at the Newsboys' Home was publishing a paper to tell about his work for the newsboys. Why couldn't Father Tim publish a magazine devoted to the wandering workmen? Yes, a magazine was the answer, a magazine which would tell the light and dark sides of their homeless lives in verse, in fiction, in humor, and in serious reflection. In September, 1908, *Father Dempsey's Hotel Record* was born and the busy pastor and hotel manager became an editor.

This would be no ordinary appeal magazine of little literary value. His thorough training at St. Mary's Seminary in Mullingar, at the diocesan seminary of Meath in Navan, and at St. Patrick's College in Carlow had given him a refined literary taste which the magazine would reflect. His articles and editorials were characterized by a vigorous and fluent style, charged with emotion and imagination, and permeated by a delicate sense of humor.

He loved to dictate letters and articles to his secretary. As the words poured out of his mouth, he would nervously tie and untie his shoestrings. Whenever he read a poem or an article he liked, he would save it for "the paper." Topics treated in its pages ranged from "Christian Marriage and Divorce," "Ireland as the Teacher of Europe," "Washington and the Irish People," "Alcohol and the Community," to "Give the Fireman His Due," "The Mail Carriers' Sunday Off," "The Policeman on Our Block," and "What's the Matter with St. Louis?" Moreover, there were articles on Father Tim, the institutions he founded, and phases of the work, numerous poems, occasional pages of jokes, and even household recipes. Everything from paint to mortician's services was advertised.

The office in the rectory was a busy place on the day that the magazines arrived from Father Dunne's print shop. The addressograph hummed as the secretary and four boys from the Newsboys' Home prepared to send out the hundreds of copies to all parts of the world. A big exchange list helped to supply the hotel recreation room with reading matter. Within a year of its foundation the magazine assumed the permanent name, *Father Dempsey's Hotel Magazine.*

Anyone connected with the editorial department of a paper or magazine will appreciate the difficulties of editing a monthly magazine. The paper may be the editor's pride and joy but it's also his headache. The man who said, "I never had a plan in my life," didn't worry too much about planning his magazine for next year or two years from now; it was headache enough to think about next month or two months from now. More important even than magazine planning was the task which engaged Father Dempsey's attention in the spring of 1909.

Chapter 3

THE EXILES' REST

DEATH plays no favorites; death is no respecter of persons. The finding of sanctuary in Father Dempsey's Hotel for Workingmen did not guarantee a drink at the fountain of youth. Many of the men who called Father Tim's their home had one leg in the grave when they registered. Here a hacking cough and blood-spitting announced consumption; there a florid countenance and labored breathing told of high blood pressure; here a jaundiced skin advertized a badly functioning gall bladder. This one complained of his rheumatism, that one of his arthritis, this one of his stomach pains, and that one of weakness and dizziness. The catalogue of diseases that rolled off the Divine press with the commission of original sin was no stranger to the hotel.

Father Tim's concern about the health of his guests manifested itself in providing hospital attention for those who needed it. The doors of hospitals under religious and secular auspices flew open to admit men from his hotel. For the hospital sisters he had the highest esteem and called them "God's noblest daughters." He could become eloquent about nurses. "Now, take the nurses," he would say. "How I do admire that class of people. Those beautiful young women, gifted, educated, fit to shine in any society, who give up their lives to relieve pain and suffering." His elevated mind could invest a vocation with a subtle beauty often missed by those closest to the vocation.

Hospital attention couldn't save the lives of some of his men. During a two-year period, January 1907 to January

1909, thirty-two of them died. For the fourteen who had no relatives or friends Father Tim provided decent burial in various cemeteries. Realizing, however, that this corporal work of mercy would continue into the future, he began to think of securing a burial lot in Calvary Cemetery. For one thing it would be more economical, and then again Father Tim mused, "I'll put them all together so they'll all get up in a bunch and maybe say a good word for me when the trumpet blows."

The Board of Directors of Calvary was sympathetic to his charitable plan. They donated a burial lot in section fifteen with dimensions of thirty by forty feet, space for one-hundred graves. When this was filled in the course of time, they donated another lot in section twenty-three. For each interment a two-dollar charge was made to help defray the expense of grave digging, bookkeeping, and footstone buying. It was the generous custom of the Bensiek-Niehaus Funeral Home to furnish the caskets and hearses free of charge. Father Tim could think of no more appropriate title for the burial place than "The Exiles' Rest." For the men buried there, life's fitful fever was over; they had gone home. And over each pile of fresh dirt Father Tim would whisper the fervent prayer, "May he rest in peace."

This new charity stirred the emotions of people. In an age which was showing less and less reverence for the dead, it was refreshing to see such a reverential concern about even the dead poor. Teresa Brayton, a poet of New York city, pronounced the judgment that "One of the most beautiful monuments to humanity is Father Tim Dempsey's 'Exiles' Rest' in Calvary Cemetery, St. Louis, where the friendless poor may find a final shelter unscathed by the shadow of public charity." So impressed was she that she devoted her poetic talents to the composition of a poem that tells the story of the men buried there. This poem, two stanzas of which are quoted here, achieved a wide popularity among the friends of Father Tim.

From roads that were hard and dreary,
  From ways that were walked in vain,
From toils that had long been weary,
  From scourgings of sun and rain;
From the empty path of the friendless
  That leadeth to no man's breast
They have found the peace that is endless,
  Asleep in the 'Exiles' Rest'. . . .

And this was the crown of their living,
  The guerdon they craved for most, —
An Irish priest for their shriving
  And peace at the utmost post;
A grave where the public finger
  Of charity writes no crest.
But ever the angels linger
  To hallow the 'Exiles' Rest'.

Since these friendless poor had not died in despair but comforted by their hope in Christ, Father Tim thought it appropriate to place a cross in "The Exiles' Rest." Only in view of the cross of Christ and the open tomb on Easter could one ask with St. Paul, "O death, where is thy victory? O death, where is thy sting?" Father Tim had a weakness for Celtic crosses. They had been a common sight for him in the cemeteries of Ireland. On many a hillside and in many a ruined abbey they marked hallowed ground where saints and chiefs had worshiped God. They rose over the exiles' graves on far-famed battlefields where the destinies of nations were decided. They had never been prostituted to glorify the vulgar wealth and pomp and power that trod on the hearts of the free. For four-hundred and fifty dollars he secured a ten-foot cross of Bedford stone. Where cross-bar met upright were the interlaced raised capital letters, "IHS," declaring for all the world that Jesus the Son of God was Saviour, and on its sloping base one could read the simple inscription, "The Exiles' Rest."

This cross would be the silent witness of the many acts of charity implied in the simple deposition of the worn-out bodies of humble men. Through rain and snow, through summer's burning sunshine and winter's gray, it would stand, a glorious symbol of Christ's passion, death, and resurrection, a comforting symbol of hope and confidence. No one knows how many shared the sentiments of that writer who climaxed his appraisal of "The Exiles' Rest" by saying, "The winds which now moan their requiems to the dying year in this silent city of the dead shall never visit a spot of earth dedicated to a sweeter sentiment nor typifying a stronger spirit of human brotherhood than this, where the Celtic Cross adorns the Exiles' Rest."

At the funerals of his men Father Tim always offered the Holy Sacrifice of the Mass and preached a short sermon himself. He was their friend to the very last. Men from the hotel assisted at Mass and served as pallbearers. On one occasion three simple wooden caskets stood before the altar. Two of the men had died at the city hospital. Each one had gasped the short message, "Tell – Father Dempsey. He is our only – only friend." The other had died at the hotel.

These three men were among the number whom the gifted Michael Gallagher, keen observer and incisive critic, eulogized in touching verse.

They delved in the earth and they sailed the seas,
They quarried the rocks and they felled the trees,
They toiled in civilization's van
As men have wrought since the world began,
In the torrid sun and the icy blast
Till the struggle of life is ended at last.
Was their life a failure, their fate a jest,
Who slumber here in the Exiles' Rest?

Destiny had flung them wide apart
From primitive scenes to the city's heart
Ere the hope of a home and an age of ease
Had passed away like a perfumed breeze.
Then crept the chill and the gathering gloom
Portending ambition's tragic doom.
Did they live in vain or die unblest
Who moulder to dust in the Exiles' Rest?

For those whose exile was over, Father Dempsey had provided this consecrated spot in the shadow of the Celtic Cross; but there were others whose life was young and whose needs were pressing, the children of St. Patrick's parish.

Chapter 4

"SUFFER THE LITTLE CHILDREN"

FATHER DEMPSEY loved children. He liked their innocent eyes, their simple ways, their boisterous play, their pealing laughter. It was a mystery to him how any married couple would deliberately try to frustrate the birth of children. He remembered the joys of his own family life. How happy his father and mother seemed when all eleven children were gathered around them in the evening by the fireplace in their humble home in Cadamstown. There they all were in his imagination: John, Tom, Frank, Joe, Vince, Mary Kate, Sash, Agnes, Jim, and Lucy Margaret who was taken away at the age of four while Tim was studying theology at Carlow.

Like his Master and Model, who told His apostles, "Suffer the little children to come unto me," Father Tim loved children. He wasn't blind to the sacrifices involved in the education of youngsters, but he had a firm conviction that the grace of God would make those sacrifices sweet to the good-willed husband and wife. Vowed to a life of celibacy himself, he found himself more deeply immersed in the affairs of children than if he had married.

The circumstances of his parish afforded him ample opportunity to exercise his love. It was a district blessed with hundreds of children. Many were physically and spiritually underprivileged. Poor mothers, deserted by heartless husbands, or widowed by the father's untimely death, or temporarily lacking support because of the father's imprisonment or hospitalization, often came to him with tears in their eyes, asking him to place their children in a home while they worked to earn a living.

Although he fully appreciated the salutary work being done in orphanages under religious and civic auspices, he was loathe to commit orphans, half-orphans, or neglected children to such institutions because he believed in trying to keep the family circle intact at all costs. The idea was repugnant to him. Yet, at the insistence of harassed mothers he had occasionally arranged for their children to be taken care of in St. Louis institutions.

But sometimes these charitable places had to refuse petitions for admittance because of their crowded condition. In June, 1910, for example, a poor woman with two little children, one six months old, the other two years, called on Father Tim. Her husband was in jail. Could Father Tim arrange for her children to be placed in some institution? The institution which he recommended was forced to turn down his letter of petition because of insufficient accommodations.

This and similar experiences led him to think of establishing a homelike place where working mothers could leave their children for the day and then call for them in the afternoon or evening at the completion of the day's work. He knew what a joy it would be for the poor, hard-working mothers to be blessed in the evening with the smiles and caresses of their children and to have their youngsters with them for the night. His plans for a nursery and emergency home were progressing in the summer of 1910. The old police station at Seventh and Carr was soon to be abandoned in favor of a new building at Tenth and Carr. Why not use the old jail for a nursery? The thought of the transformation brought a smile to Father Tim's lips.

While negotiations were still pending with the Board of Police Commissioners, he left for a health cure in Ireland. The strain of managing the affairs of the church, school, and hotel was beginning to tell on him. His robust constitution was wearing down. He was still six feet four inches tall, but the indicator on the scales no longer flew over to the 230 pound mark. Nervousness and scrupulosity were taking their toll. The doctor and Father Tim both felt that what he needed was the scent of the wild woodbine in his nostrils, the sound of the thrushes and gold-finches in his ears, and the sight of the old purplish haze hanging over the low Slieve Bloom mountains. These would be more welcome, for a time at least, than the smell of train and factory smoke, of horses, and dusty streets; than the sound of horseshoes on cobblestones, of shrill voices of angry women, and of peddlers selling their wares; than the sight of dull red-brick tenements, of straggling commission houses, and of lumbering vehicles. Yes, the home country was what he needed.

Just before his departure the parish held a farewell party for him. After songs had been sung, informal greetings exchanged, and the purse of 250 dollars presented by Mr. John McInerney, Father Dempsey, "so deeply touched by all the evidences of love and respect in which he was held by his parishioners and friends that he was scarcely able to respond at all," finally regained his composure enough to thank all and to express his love for the old parish. "Although in the minds of some my station in life as pastor of this old parish of St. Patrick's is a humble one, yet no neighboring parish, no matter how grand, no mission, no matter how exalted, nay, not even the bishop's robes, could induce me, dear friends, to leave you.

"This fact is brought home to me tonight more forcibly than ever before. Tonight on the eve of my departure on a visit to the scenes of my childhood and early manhood, I realize more fully than ever before what this old parish really is to me, and what the parishioners, both those who permanently reside here and those who are guests at the hotel, really feel for me, and I assure you, my dear friends, that down deep in my heart that feeling is reciprocated many times over.

"May God spare me to return to you better fitted than ever before to minister to your wants. And in leaving you, though only for a comparatively short time, I can truthfully say I do not do so without a feeling of regret, glad as I am of the opportunity now given through your own kindness and generosity of visiting for the first time in eleven years the land of my birth and the birthplace of many of those present here tonight or of their parents before them —Old Ireland."

The stay in Ireland was as refreshing as a rain after two weeks of dry, torrid weather. His loving parents were gone, but a thousand comforting associations hovered like good angels around their humble graves. How his father, Thomas Henry Dempsey, a civil engineer and superintendent of public works, used to love to narrate in dramatic fashion the exploits of the ancient "O'Dinasaigh" or "O'Dempsey" clan! In the twelfth century the O'Dempseys, chiefs of Clanmaliere, had led the clans in Kildare and Offaly to a smashing victory over powerful Anglo-Norman forces under Strongbow and Robert de Quincy. How the white stone walls of the sprawling old home used to shake to the tunes of all the rebel songs and ballads.

If his father and mother could only re-live with him the incidents of his boyhood and young manhood! They would see him walking to the trout stream with his spry grandfather and reaching under the rocks to catch the slippery fish; they would see the proud smile on his face as he showed them the catch. They would see him with staff in hand starting his hike for the Slieve Bloom mountains and would watch him dragging his weary legs home again. They would see him leaving for the seminary as they shed tears of mingled joy and regret and would embrace him as he returned for summer vacation. They would see their boy becoming a young man. They would smile as they remembered his pride at his skill in carving, a "fine art" he had learned at Carlow along with such lesser arts as handball and hurling. They would weep again as they pictured their son, now Father Tim, saying his first Mass at the little church in Cadamstown. His mother, Bridget Ryan, had been the first child baptized here.* His priestly blessing, *Benedictio Dei omnipotentis,* would ring again in their ears. They would remember their heartaches as they bade their missionary son good-by, their own young St. Columcille. But enough of retrospect; life had to be lived now. He would say good-by to his relatives and friends, quit the gooseberries and golf, take his sisters, Mary Kate, Sash, and Agnes with him, and hasten back to his poor.

When he returned in September, he found out that the old Carr Street station had been sold to a firm of spaghetti manufacturers. He began to look around the neighborhood for another building, and acquainted his friends, rich and poor, Catholic and non-Catholic, with his plans for a nursery. The same group that had backed his efforts to open the hotel for men promised their support in the new venture. Numerous society ladies manifested unusual interest in the nursery. A two-story brick rooming house about a block south of the church finally became the nursery and emergency home after the transformation worked by carpenters, plasterers, plumbers, and painters.

Father Tim had not rushed into this new responsibility blindly. He realized that the supervision of such a home was a worry. The problem of money, as ubiquitous as the air and as persevering as a plague, would be there to turn his gray hairs white. The problem of personnel was a delicate one demanding the exercise of tact and prudence. But God's providence had not failed in the past; why should it fail now?

The day of the formal opening and reception was a day of consolation for Father Tim and for those who had cooperated with him in realizing his dream. He was proud to introduce his director, Dr. Mary L. Lewis of the Queen's Daughters, and her assistant, Miss Mamie Reardon, to the hundreds of

---

*Father Tim later gave a new altar to this church. His brother Tom bequeathed a chalice with which his nephew, Aloysius Dempsey, said his first Mass there in the 1930's.

men and women who came to inspect the altered and renovated building. He was as busy as a sight-seeing guide, showing the visitors the reception room on the first floor in the front and the emergency section in the rear for those children who needed care day and night until they could be permanently placed with some family, and the upper floor used for the small children left by their mothers in the morning and called for in the evening. The few youngsters in the home didn't seem especially happy about having their privacy invaded by curious grownups.

In his reception talk Father Dempsey thanked all those present and all who had contributed to the fund for the establishment of the nursery. He spoke of the strong mother love in the heart of the workingwoman and explained that the purpose of the nursery was to preserve that loving heart from the agony of yielding her child or children to the permanent care of some institution or to the hands of some stranger. Reminding his listeners of the impossibility of making the nursery self-sustaining, since only a nominal fee of five cents a day was charged and in some cases nothing was asked, he expressed his conviction that the people of St. Louis would constantly lend their financial support.

Only three months after the formal opening it was evident that larger quarters were needed. The nursery had been taking care of an average of forty children daily. The former rooming house shook with the giggles and bawling of vigorous youngsters; the old house had been rejuvenated by the presence of young life. It is not improbable that the noise of the children facilitated Father Tim's purchase of the two-story architectural oddity next door, in his quest for space. Through the medium of the May issue of his *Hotel Magazine* Father Tim announced:

> There are at present eighty-three children in the Nursery every day, and we need not say that it costs money to care for such a large number of little ones. Besides the children who are brought here by their mothers to be cared for during the day, forty-seven have been sent by

the Juvenile Court and twenty-two by a non-Catholic Mission School. Although our Hotel and Nursery expenses amount to between fifteen-hundred and two-thousand dollars per month, we have been able to maintain both without incurring debt.

Debt was one of the two things he feared most of all; the other was sin. One could get rid of sin by confession, he used to say, but debt was hard to dismiss. As long as he could win the support of charitable friends, he could keep debt away from his door.

It was about this time that Father Dempsey came into contact with a pioneer type of investigator that gave a bad name to pioneer social service. This was the "Lady Bountiful" or "Key-hole" type of social investigator who would with a magnanimous gesture give one dollar to the needy in order to get five dollars worth of personal satisfaction after they had mortified the recipient almost to death by a formidable series of ill-advised, tactless, and embarrassing questions. Some of these well-meaning people merely amused Father Dempsey. They would ask him about the men at the hotel. Yes, he provided them with lodging and recreational facilities. Did he see to it that they took a bath frequently? Father Tim would sputter in feigned astonishment at this question and with devastating sarcasm ask the prim ladies, "What! Do you want me to kill them?" He was impatient with the so-called scientific methods of such investigators and used to declare with a good deal of emphasis, "I can wash ten babies while they're deciding what soap to use."

The annoying habits of some of the investigators invited the following jerky but candid excoriation: "We care for the babies of the poor women who are forced by circumstances to go away from home in order to earn enough to keep body and soul together, and were it not for a place such as we are conducting at 1017–1019 North Sixth Street, many of them would either lose the companionship of their loved little ones or would be without work the greater portion of the time and in consequence both mothers and children hungry. Both of these objects we accomplish without worry or annoyance of any kind to ourselves, without any card-index system or red-tape investigations, and we thank God that we still have enough confidence in human nature to allow ourselves to be guided as to whether a man or woman is deserving or not, by the impressions they make on us individually, without having to call a meeting of 'the board' every time we have an application for aid at either of our institutions before we can decide whether the applicant is worthy of assistance or not."

The only card-index Father Dempsey kept was in the secret recesses of his own memory. He was outspoken in his detestation of the impersonal methods of social boards.

After Mrs. Anna E. Wolkewitz became head supervisor, a kindergarten was organized by Mrs. T. J. Barnidge and others of the Queen's Daughters and put under the direction of the Misses McCabe, Koche, and Jannese. The youngsters were taught neatness and accuracy by drawing, cutting, and sewing. A piano was installed and the little ones learned to march to the music. Twenty-five tables and chairs, such as the Seven Dwarfs might have used, were furnished for them. It was Father Tim's delight to walk in on the youngsters at their games or at their study of picture books and other simple lessons. From the tiniest blubbering bit of humanity to the most loquacious five-year-old there was a smile of recognition.

Some of the mothers who confided their children to St. Patrick's were victims of desertion by their flighty husbands. If there was any person in the world that Father Tim would want to flog, it was a wife deserter. His ideal of marriage and family life was so exalted that he could scarcely find sufficiently strong words to express his fervent disgust for a man who would drag matrimony in the mud by deserting his wife and children. In one of his searing editorials on this abuse he points out that "from an actual record kept of the callers amongst the women who have come to our office asking about the details of our Day Nursery and Emergency Home . . . we find that since the twenty-third of July up to August third, twenty-four of these poor souls had been deserted by their husbands, and these same twenty-four women were left with fifty-seven children, ranging in age from three weeks to fourteen years, to support and care for."

How many deserted wives heard Father Tim's quaint expression of friendly good-by as they emerged from the parish rectory with a new grip on themselves and a strangely unfamiliar optimism, "Sure, whenever you want the sight of a friend's face, come in again, ma'am." As the woman walked down the steps, he would say in an aside, " 'Tis the heart of a beast that could leave her so." And as he looked pityingly at the child in her arms, he would remark, " 'Tis the soul of an oyster that could leave that lovely child. I read of a man they brought back for robbing a post office. What's robbing a post office alongside of deserting them? They ought to search the world over for those fellows."

If the nursery was a worry and a heavy financial burden, it was also a consolation. Letters of gratitude from mothers made Father Tim feel sure that the work was worth every sacrifice. The reason for his conviction may appear from the following typical letter:

Dear Father Dempsey:

You may be surprised to hear from me after my having not written for so long a time. Well, Father, I want to tell you that, since I got the children back from the Nursery and through your influence my husband and I made up, and started house-keeping again, we have been getting along all right.

John has been doing better than he ever has since after the first year we were married, and I firmly believe that it is all due to the influence your several talks had on him. We both of us feel that we can never thank you enough, not only for caring for the children the way you did when I had to go out to work, but for causing us both to see the mistake we were making, and advising us to fix up our differences and start life over again for our own sakes and especially for the effect our separation would have on our children's after-life.

I cannot help but wonder sometimes how you keep up as you do, always doing something for someone in trouble. I met many women while the children were in the Nursery who spoke of you as having been the means of making life worth living to them, and, although at the time I thought I was as bad off as a person could be and live, I can now realize that many of these poor souls were in a much worse condition than I. Surely God will reward you bountifully for all your kindness here on earth to His poor, misguided creatures.

Father, pray for us sometimes that we may continue as we have started, and that nothing shall ever again occur to break up our little family. John joins me in wishing you the best of luck, and Georgie (you remember him, perhaps; he is the oldest boy) wants me to tell Father Dempsey that he is coming to see him sometime and give him something for the poor little children at his Nursery. You know, he was there at Christmas time and he never forgets what an enjoyable day it was for all of those little ones, many of whom, except for your goodness, would most likely have known nothing of Christmas at all.

May God bless you and prosper you in your noble work is the prayer of . . ."

Father Dempsey always tried to make Christmas especially memorable. Sometimes Archbishop Glennon was present to watch the happy youngsters receive their presents near the huge gift-covered tree. Boys and girls from the parish school sang and presented a tableau of the Bethlehem cave scene. A flesh-and-blood child from the nursery impersonated the Babe in the manger. During the Christmas holidays and at other times singers, dancers, musicians, slide operators, and later movie operators helped to provide the children with wholesome entertainment. Father Tim believed in utilizing the resources of the community.

But it was not long before experience in the operation of the nursery persuaded him that it was necessary to make more demands on the resources of the community in the foundation and operation of another hotel. This time there would be question of women only.

Chapter 5

A HOMELIKE HOTEL FOR WOMEN

FATHER DEMPSEY'S understanding of women was guided by what his faith taught him about the Blessed Mother of God. She was full of grace and blessed among women. Through her mankind's Saviour came into the world; she was co-redeemer with Christ. Because of her dignity, sanctity, and glory she deserved to be honored. Father Tim's worn rosary gave evidence of his conviction. Her ecclesiastical feasts were celebrated in St. Patrick's church with all the ceremony and display that a poor parish could afford. His devotion to the Mother of God showed itself in a very practical way by his attitude of reverence to all women. More than once he was heard to refer to this or that woman mentioned in conversation, "Isn't she a wonderful lady? She is like the Blessed Virgin."

A famous "Toast to Woman," composed by the poet-scout, Jack Crawford, touched the sentimental streak in Father Tim:

> I shall try to drink a toast to Woman . . . in God's life-giving water, pure as her chastity, clear as her intuitions, bright as her smile, sparkling as the laughter of her eyes, strong and sustaining as her love. In the crystal water I will drink to her, that she remain queen-regent in the empire she has already won, grounded as the universe in love, built up and enthroned in the homes and hearts of the world.
>
> "I will drink to her, the full-blown flower of creation's morning, . . . to her who in childhood clasps our little hands and teaches us the first prayer to the great All-Father; who comes to us in youth with good counsel and advice, and who, when our feet go down into the dark shadows, smooths the pillow of death as none other can; to her who is the flower of flowers, the pearl of pearls, God's last but God's best gift to man — woman, peerless, pure.

For a man with the spirit of prayer such a reverential habit of mind toward women was a safeguard of his chastity. Not all the women in the neighborhood of St. Patrick's were of sound or spotless character. Plenty of them were Magdalens who hadn't yet wept, poured precious ointment on the feet of Christ, and dried them with their hair. But there were hundreds of poor, decent working women and housewives. It was the condition of these decent working women that challenged the initiative and courage of Father Dempsey.

He knew that there were unmarried working women and girls who had no home, could not afford expensive lodgings, and did not want to risk their virtue and reputation in cheap rooming houses. He knew, too, that conscientious women and girls sometimes found themselves in temporary financial distress and needed a home where they could reside comfortably and securely. He knew, moreover, that many innocent young girls and women, lured from the rural districts by the false hope of high-salaried jobs in the big city and then shocked by the grim harshness of urban life, needed the safeguards of a good hotel under respectable auspices.

This need was emphasized by a bit of experience in the management of the nursery and emergency home. Daily he was asked by mothers who wanted to leave their children at the nursery whether he could not find living quarters for them downtown close to their work and their children so that they might save the money which would otherwise be spent for carfare. The homes operated by the sisters or by benevolent organizations were either too far from the scene of daily work or were overcrowded. Why not open a homelike hotel in the parish?

After securing the approval of the archbishop, Father Tim began to search for a building. Father John Clooney, Father Tim's assistant, learned through a friend that the owners of the three-story Bement Hotel, located on the northeast corner of the Broadway and Dickson intersection, wanted to dispose of their interests and retire from business. No doubt, the pressure of the railroads and commission houses to the east persuaded them of the wisdom of such a move. Since the hotel building had many good points to recommend it, within forty-eight hours Father Tim closed the negotiations with the owners and posted a sign, "St. Patrick's Hotel for Workingwomen, Rev. Timothy Dempsey, Manager."

Renovation and alteration preceded the formal opening on July 24, 1911. Articles in the religious and secular press explained the nature and purpose of the new work and pictures of Father Dempsey and the hotel were published. Comments were made on the originality of his latest venture and the courage shown in essaying the establishment and operation of yet another institution and his confidence in God and men as to the matter of financial support.

From the start an effort was made to create a "homey" atmosphere and spirit. Father Tim realized that the spirit would depend a great deal on the matron. His choice for matron was a young Irish woman, named Mary Coughlin, whose experience as a confectionery clerk had taught her how to deal with people. The guests regarded themselves as members of a big family; and even though individuals would come and go, this family spirit persisted. The few women who stayed for years constituted a nucleus for the perpetuation of this spirit which helped to make life pleasant. If one of the "family" fell sick, the rest visited her, read to her, brought little gifts, and in other ways showed that they regarded her as one of themselves. The sick and the temporarily unemployed were allowed to remain in residence without charge.

Because the hotel accommodated any woman or girl temporarily in need of help, the impression shortly became fixed in the minds of many people that it was a refuge or home for those who were unable to help themselves and that all of those staying at the hotel were dependents. In vigorous language Father Dempsey refuted this charge in the pages of his *Hotel Magazine:*

It is not a home for ne'er-do-wells, it is not a refuge, and the people whose names appear on the registers of both of our hotels are those who have just as much pride, are just as independent (even though poor in this world's goods), and think just as much, if not more, of their good names, as any of the guests of the hotels where they are paying as much per day for their accommodation as we charge our guests for a week.

The hotel prospectus advertized that "Rooms, neatly furnished, well ventilated and lighted," would be available "for from one dollar to one and one half dollars per week. Beds in large, spacious dormitory, seventy-five cents a week."

In addition it offered the inducements of: "books, magazines, daily papers, piano and music, stationery, employment through free labor agency, safe in office for valuables, telephone service."

Finally it provided, as did the men's hotel: "good, wholesome, well-cooked meals, composed of the best grade of meats, groceries and vegetables the market affords, for five, ten, and fifteen cents. Perfect service is assured. Can you beat it?"

During the first five months one-hundred and fifty different guests were entertained, to use the language of Father Tim; 7960 meals were served, 500 of them free; employment was secured for seventy-five; and six were sent to hospitals free of charge. One of the guests told a reporter for a St. Louis daily, "We may be bad or blue when we come to the hotel, but we never stay that way. I don't know how Father Dempsey manages it, but, if he were not such a good man, I'd say he had witch powers. Nobody can stay bad and stay in the hotel at the same time."

One guest who arrived feeling very sad and blue expressed her feelings about the hotel in moving verses entitled "A Shelter in the Time of Storms." They made such an impression on Father Tim that he published them in the *Hotel Magazine*. Through all their crudeness we catch the authentic cry from the depths of a crushed soul, alone in the desolation of a large city.

O city, you are big and your eyes are bright,
But your vision of life is small,
When you see not the bursting of a human heart
Nor hear its mournful call,
As it tosses back to the Infinite
His wonderful gift of life.

The temptation to suicide is then described, as she pictures herself looking on the glistening expanse of the Mississippi. But her heart turns to God.

How awful, in the silent universe,
To be driven to the point that breaks,
When we doubt the Father's pitying love
And wonder why He forsakes!

Then extremity's cry from the depth of my soul,
Where earthly hopes lay bleeding,
Spontaneously rose from a broken heart.
God heard its sorrowful pleading.

There now follows the account of how He led her to this refuge, this shelter, "where one needs not the golden key," but the latch flies up at the gentlest knock:

And sheltered from the cold outside,
Beneath the smile of God,
The tired one forgets her ache
And the weary path she's trod.

Life's unfortunates were not the only ones to avail themselves of the hotel's services. Sometimes very well-dressed women with more than moderate means chose to stay at the hotel. When such a woman asked for a room on one occasion, Mary Coughlin hinted that perhaps she might want another hotel which could offer better rooms and richer meals. The woman held her ground. "If you don't mind, I'll stay here. The policeman directed me here when I asked him for a place where a woman alone could go." The obliging matron was happy to receive this same woman on subsequent visits to the city.

The parish institutions often proved mutually complementary. On one occasion a woman from Gary, Ind., arrived in St. Louis with her two children late in the evening. She had expected her husband to meet her and the children at the depot. Imagine her disappointment and worry when he did not show up. Through a priest of the city she learned that her husband was ill in a St. Louis hospital. She was one of the happiest women in the world when she was told that St. Patrick's Hotel for Workingwomen would be glad to take care of her, St. Patrick's Day Nursery and Emergency Home would provide for her two children, and Father Dempsey's Hotel for Workingmen would shelter her husband after his release from the hospital and until such time as he was able to assume his former position.

A Free Labor Agency was conducted in connection with the hotel, and Miss Nellie Quick of the State Free Employment Bureau cooperated with the matron in regard to securing work. When women and girls without home and work reported to Miss Quick, she would send them to the hotel until she could find work for them. Father Dempsey himself kept an eye open for jobs for those living there. Hundreds of St. Louis families got their maids and servants at the recommendation of St. Patrick's pastor.

A long-time friend of Father Tim, former senator Harry B. Hawes, relates: "One amusing side of our friendship was the fact that all of the girls serving in our household came from Ireland, and with rare exceptions they all married policemen, and just before the marriage of each Father Tim would know about it and have some new ones for my family."

The management of the Women's Hotel, the Men's Hotel, the Day Nursery, and The Exiles' Rest was not enough for Father Tim. The year of the establishment of the Women's Hotel, 1911, also plunged him into parole work.

Chapter 6

"I WAS IN PRISON"

IT WAS only natural that criminals should wander into the precincts of St. Patrick's parish. Here were the flophouses, saloons, and dives. Here they met their friends and accomplices. The location of the city of St. Louis on a number of main railroad trunk lines invited less desirable guests from all parts of the country. Sometimes freight hoppers were so thick on the trains that railroad crews and detectives would have invited murder if they had tried to force the "free tickets" off. Occasionally a long string of sand, coal, and box cars had the appearance of a traveling I.W.W. convention. Not all these free travelers were bad. Many were just hard up. In any case, they were a problem for the police. For Father Tim they were an opportunity.

People in trouble were a specialty for Father Tim. For many years he had made it a practice to pay a daily visit to the Carr Street police station to see whether any of his men had been picked up. Captain Michael O'Malley almost despaired of converting Father Tim from his lenient attitude toward the imprisoned. When one of his own hotel guests or even a casual acquaintance got into a really serious scrape and wound up in the penitentiary for a stretch, this Irish "troubleshooter" corresponded with him and encouraged him. When the time for parole came, Father Tim would act as sponsor if he thought the man was a safe risk.

His sympathetic interest in the welfare of prisoners won for him membership on the board of directors of the Aid Society for Inmates of State Penal and Reformatory Institutions, organized in 1911. The purpose of this society was to create a fund to be used for all the requirements of a Catholic chaplain and for the relief of inmates after their discharge. By personal begging and by appeals in the pages of his *Hotel Magazine* Father Dempsey was able to contribute to this fund. He was pleased to hear from the chaplain, the Rev. Henry A. Geisert, about the spiritual improvement of the "forgotten men" after the establishment of the Holy Name Society in the state prison at Jefferson City.

With an invitation to the readers of the *Hotel Magazine* to send "any religious, or other good, solid reading matter" to the prison where "it will be carefully read by many a poor fellow who is no worse than many others on the outside who were lucky enough not to 'get caught,'" he extends his best wishes to the members of the St. Dominic's branch of the Holy Name Society and their chaplain and prays that "the good things gained from their banding together in upholding the Holy Name of Jesus may follow them through the entirety of their several lives and always be of great spiritual aid to them at all times."

Father Tim's reputation as a friend of the needy reached into the dark corners of numerous penitentiaries and reformatories. From cell to cell and from room to room the word was passed along that Father Tim Dempsey of St. Louis would act as sponsor. To men whose parole had been refused because of the inability to get a responsible sponsor, the name of Father Tim became hallowed. At mention of his name hard, tired faces, deep-lined with despair, brightened and even attempted a weary smile. Chaplains recommended parolees to him. The following letter from a chaplain of the Menard Division of the Illinois State Penitentiary, the Rev. A. F. Giesen, is typical:

Dear Father Dempsey:

Am writing these few lines to you to ask you in your kindness to sign the parole papers of an inmate by the name of . . . , who has received notice of his parole. Some relatives of friends of his have spoken to you and you informed them to have me write to you. Kindly let me know at your convenience whether you will be able or are willing to do this act of charity for this man. The necessary papers will be sent you after your reply.

Regards and best wishes.

Fraternally in Christ, . . .

This letter brought the following prompt response from Father Tim:

My dear Father Giesen:

I received your letter in regard to Mr. . . . , and upon your recommendation and that of the warden I will sign the papers of parole.

Please have Mr. . . . mail me the necessary forms at his earliest opportunity.

I beg to remain,
Fraternally yours in Christ,
(signed) Timothy Dempsey

Unless Father Dempsey knew more about a prisoner than the warden did, he would honor the warden's recommendations. A letter such as the following from the Menard warden would invariably produce prompt action in favor of the prospective parolee:

Dear Father Dempsey:

J . . . M . . . , No. . . . has given me your letter to him.

This person was received at this Institution November 10th 19. . on a charge of larceny. He has a previous history of two terms at Jefferson City, but his record at this Institution is perfect, and really I think he can be returned to society and make a good citizen.

I am making this recommendation to you in view of the above.

Very truly yours, . . .

Far from being utterly indiscriminate in accepting parolees, Father Dempsey depended heavily upon the recommendations of wardens, chaplains, parole officers, employers, and relatives.

The sponsorship of a prisoner placed on parole involves too much responsibility and work to admit of an utterly indifferent attitude as to who is committed to one's care. Letters must be written, formal blanks filled, lodging and work secured. Father Tim went out of his way to keep in contact with his parolees. His idea of having them report to him two or three times a month was an important contribution to their care. Some of them he was able to employ himself in various jobs connected with his institutions. Others he commended to farmers and to heads of business houses. Since he was a public figure and the friend of hundreds of employers, he was usually able to get jobs for his parolees. When Father Tim called an employer and said, "I have a man for you," the usual answer was, "Send him over, Father. We'll find something for him to do." And another prisoner was on the long hard road to rehabilitation.

Father Dempsey's parole work did not escape stinging darts of criticism. He was too soft-hearted; he took too big a "load" for one man; he was multiplying the criminals in St. Louis; he was butting into the business of scientific parole workers; and he was just trying to make a name for himself. These criticisms affected Father Tim about as much as a breeze affects a four-motored bomber. He realized that he made mistakes just as any other human being, but he was convinced that the work was a good one and a necessary one. The letters he received from men in institutions touched his heart and awakened his pity, not the sort of pity that Arnold Lunn describes as "an objection to being reminded of the existence of pain," but the sort of pity that the Good Samaritan showed when he rescued the bruised and bleeding victim of robbers.

The appeals he received might be crudely handwritten, beautifully penned, or neatly typed; they might be frank, whining, sentimental, or seemingly insincere; but nearly all contained a promise of amendment and expressions of a vehement desire to be released. One lad at the Boonville Training School, affiliated with the Missouri State Penitentiary, scribbled an ungrammatical, heart-stirring appeal in pencil:

> . . . Father they sent me down here for stealing 2 bicycles and got 2 years . . . my parents havent Wrote to me for about 2 months. I Think they dont want to help me out of here I have always Been a

good boy I never mistreated any one only I made a bad mistake when I stoled I should not have done that Never again will I do such deeds again but God will forgive me I know he will . . . I wish I could see you and speak to you I knew you ever since I was a baby.

A prisoner at Leavenworth, Kansas, asked Father Tim to get him a job so that he could be paroled. "And I'm sure," said he, "that this experience has taught me that crime doesn't pay." A prisoner at Joliet, Illinois, confesses, "I well know I have done wrong but I am going To do right when I get out of here." An inmate of the Illinois State Penitentiary, Menard Division, admits with a bit of naïveté, "I am tired of this kind of life. I am now in this ten years of my life gone. hope to see you soon may God able me to explain God bless you all yours in Christ."

Another prisoner at Menard pays unconscious tribute to the prison surveillance in the words, "It seams hard to get out of this place, after I have all ready served ten long years in here. no father, or mother, no sister, or Brother. Answer soon. God bless you." Besides striking a sympathetic chord, certain appeals at times startled Father Tim by their literary finish. A Menard inmate wrote, "In view of the fact that I have no relatives, nor friends, sufficiently interested to come to my assitance in this matter, I am appealing to you." A slightly veiled compliment as to his ability to find work for parolees brought a smile to the lips of Father Tim: "I am writing to you upon the suggestion of some friends of mine in regards to signing my parole. Now Mr. Dempsey I have sent 4 sets of papers out and have failed so far the reason being no work."

A long-term inmate professed to know of Father Tim's reputation for kindness: "Knowing of your many kind deeds to unfortunates, I am writing to seek your assistance in obtaining my liberation. I have been in this prison for over 21 years, and have lost contact with people in the outside world." Another long-term prisoner, a young man of twenty-seven and a half years, confessed to Father Tim: "I have made a bad mistake by going around with older boys than myself, at the time I got in this trouble I was only 18 years old. I wante to come out and make Some thing out of my self. my mother is getting old and needs my help. if you will sign my Parole I will promise to never get in any trouble and never cause you to have any regrets for helping me get out."

Not all the parolees who made such fervent promises were as good as their word. Some of them broke faith with him and caused him grief and trouble. The delinquency of a few was so serious that they found themselves back in prison. But Father Tim believed that the pile of gold refined from the dross was worth an occasional headache and heartache.

He proved himself the prisoner's friend without inviting any such castigation as that hurled from the sneering lips of an embittered prisoner in one of our state penitentiaries after a fellow prisoner had just said, "I have been giving [things] away all my life." In retort the embittered cell mate cynically and triumphantly psychoanalyzed: "Now I get your number. You are one of those charitable guys that only think they are charitable; always wanting to be on the giving end; deadly afraid of being under obligation to the other fellow. Did you ever give a thought to the fact that it may do the other guy some good to be a giver too? Guys like you, nine times out of ten, are only satisfying their own conceit. Always want to be the philanthropist; rather starve than give the other guy a chance to feel smug like themselves. You'd give a guy a buck, get two bucks' worth of kick out of it, and then pat yourself on the back for your charitableness."

Father Dempsey was no mere philanthropist. Though born of the same sentiment, philanthropy and charity are as different as night and day. In the words of the Very Rev. A. P. Doyle, C.S.P., "Christian charity, born in Heaven, leads back to the land beyond the stars; philanthropy is born on earth and seldom reaches beyond the stars. Philanthropy divides among the wrecks of humanity the wealth that cannot be taken beyond the grave; charity divides among fellow men Christian love which is eternal."

His charity was especially stirred by the plight of the prisoner condemned to death. On more than one occasion he hurried to Jefferson City by train in order to intercede for some poor fellow whom he judged undeserving of the death penalty. For the condemned man's comfort he might tell the story of the only Saint who was canonized before he died, the story of St. Dismas or the Good Thief. Crucified on Calvary alongside the Saviour of the world, Dismas groaned, "Lord, remember me when Thou shalt come into Thy kingdom." The dying Christ rewarded his faith and contrition by complete forgiveness of his black load of sins: "Amen I say to thee, this day thou shalt be with Me in paradise." Dempster MacMurphy, late business manager of the *Chicago Daily News,* called this patron Saint of the condemned a "hoodlum saint, who roams the outfield of eternity, making shoestring catches of souls – a saint who has no following to speak of, no medals, no propaganda."

At St. Patrick's this "hoodlum saint" had a following, especially after Father Tim secured a statue of him and placed it just inside the entrance of the church. He hoped to encourage sinners to strive for sanctity. The drunks were a special worry. Even short-term pledges couldn't keep some of them out of jail. Sometimes Father Tim would almost run out of patience with the habitual drunkard.

One day as he and another priest approached the Men's Hotel, a drunk was to be seen clinging to a lamp post in front of the hotel. Father Tim touched his companion on the wrist and pointing to the poor fellow remarked, "See the great help prohibition is to sobriety." He pulled the drunken man to a vertical position alongside the lamp post. The drunk's bleary eyes opened wide as his alcohol-soaked brain tried to comprehend the sharp order ringing in his ears, "You blackguard, you. Go up and get to bed." The man needed help. Father Dempsey guided the man's staggering steps across the red brick sidewalk and up the worn flagstones.

His first comment as he resumed the conversation with his

interested priest friend revealed a flash of his love for God and for broken humanity, "Thank God for making the lamp post; it keeps them out of the gutter." Then after a long pause, he added, "Broken china, Father, broken china. Some there are who think it time wasted to work for such as these. But out in Calvary, Father, out in Calvary I have laid away in our little plot many a one of them. Outcasts maybe in the eyes of men, but in the eyes of God noblemen. For they went across fortified by the grace-giving Sacraments of their Mother the Church. Even if they have to wait a while, before too long they will be let in. Some of them, I trust, perhaps many of them are already there. Father, that's worth while don't you think?"

His priest friend nodded as he realized he was talking to a one-man salvage corporation for wrecked spiritual lives. The intemperate were indeed broken china.

Father Dempsey's efforts to help the intemperate sometimes put him in embarrassing positions. One evening a wiry old lady, an habitual sponge, was having a hard time keeping her feet from tangling as she tried to cross the street. Father Tim put his arm in her arm and began to lead her across. Halfway across, the drunken woman slipped and pulled him down with her. As the two sat there in the middle of the street, arm in arm, the drunken woman looked at her clerical escort through bloodshot eyes and in a tone of compassion asked, "Are you hurt, Father?" "No," he replied, "just embarrassed."

He could stand a bit of embarrassment himself, but when drunks began to embarrass the Saints, he could be very firm. One day he heard somebody shouting in the church. He hastened to see the cause of the commotion. A ragged man, standing in front of the statue of St. Joseph near the Communion rail, was staring at the benign figure of the Saint, and with right arm upraised and fist clenched was shouting in half-drunken fashion, "If you're a man, come down from there!" Although the poor man had reached the belligerent stage of drunkenness, Father Dempsey was able to persuade him that St. Joseph was a peace-loving man and his friend.

When drunks tried to corrupt the young, Father Tim could charge the atmosphere with lightning bolts from his sharp tongue and give an example of muscular Christianity. It was First Communion day. Led by banner bearers, the boys and girls, all dressed in white, were marching around the block before entering the church for Mass. Father Tim was riding behind them in a carriage pulled by a team of well-groomed horses. As the procession reached the corner, a group of half-drunk ruffians began to guffaw and ridicule the solemn proceedings. Father Tim's blood began to boil. Waving a bucket of beer, one half-drunk ruffian shouted an invitation to the frightened youngsters, "Come on and have a drink."

Father Dempsey didn't wait to open the carriage door. Over the side he leaped. Plunging into the drunken band, he pounded them and scattered them with his big fists and added a stinging tongue-lashing.

He was accustomed to offer extrinsic inducements to convert some of the men from their drinking ways. A certain Denny was such a one. A skilled mechanic, Denny could have been making good money if it were not for the bewitching power of the spigot. Finally Father Tim said, "Now listen, Denny, if you'll stop drinkin' for six months, I'll give you a check for fifty dollars at the end of that time."

"Ah, if I stopped that long," snapped Denny, "I could write you a check for one-hundred, Father."

Sometimes Father Dempsey had the consolation of seeing an inveterate drinker give up his bad habit. Especially was this true in the latter years when he could point to the heroic example of the Dublin lumberman, Matt Talbot, whose early self-indulgence was atoned for by a laborious and penitential life. He gave away hundreds of copies of a short biography of this drinking sinner who became a sober and saintly man.

A certain Pat was one of those who had conquered his bad habit. One hot night in August Father Tim was sitting on the front steps of the church. His collar was off and he was in shirt sleeves. A full moon smiled in the cloudless heavens. Its light seemed to sublimate the sordid surroundings. Father Tim was staring at the double ring around the moon when white-haired Pat happened along.

" 'Tis a beautiful night, isn't it, Pat?"

"It is that, Father."

"But, Pat, have you noticed the two rings about the moon?"

Old Pat looked up, squinted for a minute, then said solemnly, "You know, Father, I don't see rings around the moon any more since I quit drinking."

Such snappy comebacks pleased Father Tim almost as much as the honesty of the man who walked up to him and asked for a quarter for a drink. The man got the quarter. Temperate drinkers did not fall under his censure. After all, he himself did not disdain the stimulation afforded by a mint julep, a highball, or a glass of sparkling champagne. He did not share the belief of prohibitionists that temperance could be forced on people by external laws; he knew that restraint had to come from the interior. He knew, too, that the supernatural virtue of temperance could be maintained only by the help of grace. His system of reclaiming drunks differed basically from the system of Alcoholics Anonymous. The natural means, however, were not ignored.

His appointment to the board of directors of the Aid Society for Inmates of State Penal and Reformatory Institutions in 1911 had formally launched him on a lifelong career of rehabilitating prisoners.

But there were still other and most serious problems confronting him. In these, his long acquaintance with workingmen was to stand him in good stead. Beginning with 1915, Father Tim was to prove himself to be of invaluable help in the settlement of industrial disputes.

Chapter 7

A ONE MAN DISPUTE COMMISSION

THE election of Woodrow Wilson to the presidency of the United States in 1912 ushered in an era of momentous change in the life of Americans. The Underwood-Simmons Bill embodied the Democratic principle of lowering tariffs. The Federal Reserve Act aimed to reconcile the banks and the people. The Federal Trade Commission was organized to represent the government in its supervision of trusts. A separate Department of Labor appeared with jurisdiction over the old Bureau of Labor, immigration, naturalization, and the Children's Bureau. The Seamen's Bill for improving the conditions of sailors in the merchant marine was passed. Civil war in Mexico provoked American intervention. From a policy of neutrality in 1914, the year of the outbreak of World War I, the United States passed to active participation on the side of the Allies in 1917. The Federal Government assumed wider powers.

Father Dempsey was not blind to these changes. He was not buried in his little world at St. Patrick's. His was a cosmopolitan outlook. His was the view expressed by Karl Adam that "mankind must not be regarded as a mass of homogeneous beings successively emerging and passing away, nor merely as a sum of men bound together by unity of generation, as being descendants of one original parent, but as one single man. So closely are men assimilated to one another in their natural being, in body and in mind, so profoundly are they interlocked in thinking, willing, feeling, and acting, so solidary is their life, their virtue and their sin, that they are considered in the divine plan of redemption only as a whole, only as a unity, only as one man."

The pastor of St. Patrick's hated to see even the superficial unity of international peace smashed by war. He hated to hear of the miniature civil wars between employers and employees that threatened the happiness of millions of Americans in the years immediately preceding the entrance of the United States into World War I. But he would take an active part in the work of helping to solve in a practical way the local problems of capital and labor.

The war made it possible for organized labor to gain unprecedented victories in the struggle for social justice. With the stoppage of the yearly immigration of cheap labor from Europe, and with the growing demand for American-made goods on the part of Allied consumers, labor was in a better position to make demands of capital. Strikes were the most common weapon used. Practically every important industrial and mining region in the country suffered a series of strikes. St. Louis was no exception.

Because of his intelligent interest in the affairs of workingmen, Father Dempsey found himself waist-deep in a slough of industrial problems. As a young priest at St. John the Baptist's in Moberly and at Holy Angels' and Assumption in St. Louis, he had kept his finger on the pulse of the labor movement. His emotions had been stirred by the newspaper accounts of the strikes at the Carnegie Steel Company and the Pullman Company and the various mines. His work at St. Patrick's brought him face-to-face with local problems. He sympathized with the laboring men as underdogs in a society where cooperation had not yet supplanted class warfare and where harmony and mutual understanding between capital and labor had been sparsely fostered. For workingmen and workingwomen he had established his hotels, and for the children of the working class his day nursery and emergency home. In the pages of his *Hotel Magazine* he upheld the rights and explained the duties of workingmen.

As a member of a symposium dealing with the relation of Christianity to the workingman, he delivered a masterful speech in 1910 at Goller Hall before a thousand members of the Workingmen's Welfare Association. "The capitalist," he said, "has a superabundance of faults, and God Almighty warned him that it was as hard for him to get to heaven as it was for a camel to pass through the eye of a needle; yet, let me tell you workingmen that it's just as hard for a poor man to enter the Golden Gates if he doesn't behave himself. No doubt, the latter has not the same difficulties to contend with as the former, for gold has charmed many a beautiful life into foolish adoration at its shrine; yes, and it would invade the Sanctuary to still the voice of God's ministers who would warn the sons of men of its deceptive mien. . . . The workingmen belong to us and we belong to them. We must not be conformed to this world, but our constant effort must be in imitation of our Leader to make the world conform to our ideals. We know the truth and the truth has made us free. Our limitations are defined for us, not by any fancied whims of men, but by the unerring Church of God."

The numerous strikes at the time drew the following comment from him: "These almost continuous strikes are simply civil wars in miniature – internecine warfare of a most vicious type – and in great danger, at some time or another in the future, of leading to most disastrous results. The evils of these strikes, such as loss of life, loss of positions by honest, hard-working men, are on a level with the evils of genuine war. They have also developed a class in this country known as strikebreakers whose ranks are filled from the slums of the large cities, whose only commendation is their lack of fear, and this is due solely and wholly to their lack of conscience."

In the same speech he briefly analyzed the relation between strikes and vagrancy. "If we were asked the question what cause contributed most toward putting so many men 'on the road,' we believe from our experience we could truthfully answer, 'strikes.' Because when a man is accustomed to one line of work, and goes through a strike, it is a most difficult matter for him to get another job in the same line, and not being fitted for anything else, in many cases it drives him to the wandering life, away from home, church ties, and the rest. There should certainly be some interference on the part of the authorities, and this, too, before the riot stage of the trouble has been reached. A strike should be the very last resort for the workingman. Every effort for an amicable settlement of all differences should be made, for the sake of himself, his family, his country, and his God, before the strike method is adopted."

The attentive audience listened eagerly to his plea for harmonious cooperation. "While the Church recognizes the right and the necessity, and would foster the formation of the workingmen's unions, she asks and claims as the representative of the workingmen's model, our Lord Jesus Christ, the right to command the capitalist to take his place with the 'wise men of the East,' and the workingmen to join the shepherds, and both in union to swear allegiance to the King of the rich and poor and promise equal rights to all men of every creed and race and clime, and fair play and justice to one another. If the remembrance of that scene which was enacted around the crib at Bethlehem would only tarry sufficiently long in the minds of men to make them realize their obligations toward each other and toward their Maker, this earth would be a veritable Paradise, and peace and happiness would reign supreme."

Such exhortations may have prevented some strikes, but the number each year continued to mount until in 1915 there were almost 2000 strikes throughout the country. A strike in St. Louis during August of this same year started Father Tim on a busy career of conciliation.

On Saturday, August 14, he was shocked by the news that the teamsters had declared a strike the day before. Disturbing visions of shooting and fighting and killing flooded his imagination. He couldn't forget what happened four years earlier when Local 700 struck against a certain paper company. Two of the strikers, Paddy and Mike Kane, who despite the same name were no relation, bumped into two strikebreakers at Sixth and O'Fallon, a block north of St. Patrick's. Their fists were not equal to the revolvers of the strikebreakers. Both Paddy and Mike were carried into the rectory dying. Father Tim feared a repetition of deeds of violence. He said to himself, "Somebody ought to put a stop to this." He thought of Nellie Quick at the State Free Employment Bureau, and picked up the telephone.

"This teamster strike, Nellie. It ought to be stopped."

"Sure, Father, it ought to be stopped. Why don't you stop it?"

"Well, whom have I got to see?"

"There's John Duggan, who's business agent of the union, and Dan Murphy is seventh vice-president, and Tom Coyne president."

Father Tim thanked God for these Irish names and called up the union. Duggan was out.

"Well, who's this talkin'? . . . Oh, Danny Murphy. Well, I'm Father Dempsey. Isn't there some way we can stop this strike. I'd like to see you."

In five minutes the young and enterprising teamster leader walked into the rectory. "It would be grand," he told Father Tim during the course of their conversation, "if you could get this stopped."

"Well, who is there can stop it?" asked Father Tim.

"George Tansey, the head of the St. Louis Transfer Company."

After Murphy left, Father Tim called Tansey, "as decent a man he was – God rest him – as ever lived," in the words of Father Tim. Over a hundred freight drivers, chauffeurs, and helpers had started the strike against Tansey's company, demanding shorter working hours, and an increase in pay ranging from $1.50 to $2 a week. The strike spread to other large hauling firms, ultimately involving 1500 truck, freight, transfer, and mail drivers, chauffeurs and helpers.

Tansey and Father Dempsey threshed the whole affair out at the rectory. It was good to get the owner's slant of the strike. The leaders of both sides agreed to meet with Father Tim at the Mercantile Club that night for a conference. After all, the sufferers from the strike would be the 750,000 people in need of food, clothing, building material, and working material. A teamsters' strike in 1915 is comparable to a truck-drivers' strike now.

But during that long Saturday events seemed to conspire against a successful conference. In the vicinity of the transfer companies strikers and strikebreakers battled as often as they could elude a vigilant police detail. Wagons were overturned. Excited teams, nervously pounding the cobblestones as they seemed to sense the tension, were stampeded into a runaway gallop by the stinging lashes of sullen strikers. At Eads bridge the strikebreaking drivers were able to get through without accident only because police revolvers awed the strike sympathizers. A reporter for one of the papers was beaten and kicked when he was mistaken for a strikebreaker. With this background the evening meeting promised to be stormy.

Before leaving for the meeting, Father Tim called the Sisters at the nursery and asked them to have the children pray for the success of his peaceful mission. He knelt in prayer for a few minutes in front of the altar of St. Patrick in the church.

The friendly way in which the rival leaders debated the various issues gave Father Tim a delightful surprise. When they reached an impasse on certain matters, he suggested compromise. Finally the union leaders said they would offer the team owners' proposed agreement to the union men at a meeting on the following day. The agreement provided for the same wage scale for a period of one year and a number of changes in the working hours. Drivers were to report at the barns at 6:30 instead of six; overtime was to begin at 6:20 instead of 6:35. Men out after 6:20 were to receive pay for a full hour. No work would be done on Sunday by the drivers. A driver who was to be laid off would be told the night before. The daily newspapers in their reporting of the Saturday night meeting gave an optimistic slant which belied the fact. Father Tim was no pessimist; neither was he so sanguine as to think everything was over. His judgment was right.

At their meeting in the hall of the Central Trades and Labor Union the teamsters rejected the agreement because of the failure to include a wage concession. Murphy quickly contacted Tansey and arranged for another meeting of the two subcommittees that evening. With Father Tim acting as adviser they met in the stuffy office of the St. Louis Transfer Company. For two hours words flew back and forth. Finally the owners offered an agreement which satisfied the strikers' subcommittee. Father Dempsey and the subcommittee hurried to the union hall where hundreds of eager, sweating strikers were waiting for news. They listened to Duggan's report.

Drivers and helpers were to get a fifty cent increase per week; stablemen a two dollar increase per month and a cut in hours of work from twelve to eleven. The drivers' working time was to be cut one-half hour; there was to be no Sunday work; there would be no layoffs without warning the night before, and no wagonloads over 9000 pounds. After short talks by Murphy, Coyne, and Father Dempsey, the striking drivers unanimously accepted the agreement. The strike was over. Calamity had been averted. Father Tim breathed freely again.

"I am the happiest man in the world," he told the newspaper reporters. "I was sure that the situation could be relieved without violence if the men would only get together. . . . I never met a more gentlemanly or a finer lot of men in my life. I was treated with the greatest courtesy and kindness, and I am glad if I was any help in ending the disturbance." The downtown quarterbacks that night were saying that Father Dempsey was a bigger man than President Wilson. The newspapers attributed the averting of serious trouble to the timely and tactful intervention of Father Tim. Union leaders and officials of the team owners' association expressed their gratitude to him.

"There is not another man in St. Louis," said John Duggan, "who could have handled the situation more carefully and diplomatically than Father Dempsey." Tansey declared, "We feel that we have granted more than we should, under present business conditions, but in the interest of harmony and peace we decided to do all we could to relieve the situation."

With characteristic humility Father Tim called his part in the settlement "just an accident." "They're saying I settled the teamsters' strike. I didn't settle it. I only got the men who settled it together. . . . I didn't really say anything except to talk a very little about strikes and the harm they did, and how it was that they came from misunderstanding – just misunderstanding. I told them what happened to the Kane boys, and that if any more of the boys were killed, I shouldn't be able to sleep nights for six months."

The *St. Louis Republic* called him "the pacificator of the hour." "To him a strike is not an economic issue, but a human tragedy," ran the editorial. "He sees, not just two impersonal sides engaged in some titanic struggle; rather, two sets of men who for the moment have lost the balance of mutual understanding between man and man. . . . After everything is said and done, strikes are very human things, and blessed is the man with humanity enough to see his way clear to the human sympathies involved."

The irrepressible Michael Gallagher, who later succeeded Miss Anne Smyth as Father Tim's secretary, offered his reflections in the *Hotel Magazine:*

Father Dempsey has done far more than settle a strike. He has shown St. Louis that the city is more than a present population of 750,000 or a prospective one of a million. He has also proved that it can be a community — which is a different thing. He has by the exercise of inspired common-sense proved that the people of all classes may be molded into harmonious action for common ends and purposes.

Insisting that "Father Dempsey's popularity and prestige in Missouri cannot be considered apart from his devotion within the sanctuary of the Church," Gallagher developed the idea of the influence of the supernatural on the strike:

> No one who neglected to make the Faith the guiding star of his life could retain the mental poise, the suavity and the humor that distinguish Father Dempsey. For he never sees good times. Our imaginary radical would go insane in a month if he had to help, to hearten, pacify, mollify and eventually satisfy the disappointed, indigent and embittered lines that converge at his door from all points of the compass. And if our radical friend had never prayed before and did not know how, he would find it necessary, in the circumstances, to invent a prayer of his own in order to save his sanity from speedy collapse. Such a person cannot understand the act of the good Sisters of St. Patrick's Day Nursery in praying before the statue of the Infant Jesus of Prague in the chapel that time he was in conference with the representatives of the teamsters and their employers.

As a token of appreciation for his conciliatory services the Team Owners' Association donated over a thousand dollars to Father Tim for use in his charitable works. Plans for an industrial dispute board or a strike commission began to be aired shortly after this successful conciliation. In an interview with a reporter for the *St. Louis Republic* Father Dempsey said:

> A few days ago your paper asked whether a little organization couldn't be got together to prevent strikes and lockouts. I can't get it out of my mind. God knows they ought to be prevented. I don't know anything about the labor question in a scientific way. I never read a book about it in my life.
>
> But I know a little about keeping men from fighting. Why, since I opened my hotel, 60,000 men have stopped with me and I never had a fight in my house yet. Now down at bottom all men are the same; they want to do what is right. And strikes come about just because the men who might prevent them don't get together in time, or don't meet in the right way. . . .

Why can't we have a little organization that always would be there and always ready to bring the two sides together to talk these things over before the men walk out or are locked out? I have been wondering whether the city couldn't take this thing up. If we could have a commission appointed by the mayor to represent the public and let two members be added for each case it took up, one from the employers and one from the men, I believe we could almost put a stop to strikes in St. Louis.

The commission couldn't decide what was right in a case and make the parties stand by it. That's nonsense. But the man that says so foolish a thing doesn't understand what the real need is. It isn't to settle labor troubles for the people that are in them. It is just to bring those people together so that they will settle the troubles for themselves.

And all we would want the power of the law for, if we could have it, would be just to hold off the strike or lockout until the commission could look into the matter and report, that is, until its members could make themselves intelligent about the trouble so as to know the best way of bringing the parties together. I should like to suggest that the mayor and the city counselor be asked whether we couldn't have a bit of an ordinance drawn up to form such a commission. Wouldn't it be better than to let the strike come and have men hurt and maybe killed and women and children hungry and maybe sick and business stopped and people losing money, and all because two sets of men that could have settled the whole thing in thirty minutes didn't get together?

At the advice of Mayor Kiel the city counselor, Charles H. Daues, at once began to draft an ordinance covering Father Tim's suggestions, with the intention of introducing it to the board of aldermen. The name of the proposed commission would be the "Industrial Dispute Commission." ". . . We will be pioneers in this direction," said Daues enthusiastically, "for there is no such commission established yet in any city, to my knowledge."

But the fires of Daues' enthusiasm were quickly quenched. The parties of labor disputes were not yet ready to trust themselves to such a commission. The plan was too novel for 1915. Disputing parties would continue to call on the one-man "commission," Father Dempsey, but they wouldn't adopt his progressive plan. The age of boards of conciliation, mediation, and arbitration had not yet arrived. Strong passions and unbalanced emotions instead of calm reason would continue to sway disputants in most places. Men had not grasped the truth expressed by the psychologist, the Rev. Raphael C. McCarthy, S.J., in his book, *Safeguarding Mental Health:*

> There would surely be far fewer wars, and strikes, and discords between capital and labor, if nations and individuals would gather around tables for a calm discussion of their difficulties instead of being swept into conflict by their passions.

At the very time that he was being acclaimed as the pacificator of the hour, Father Tim was almost a nervous wreck from worrying about finances. Money wasn't coming in as fast as it was running out. He could still get help from personal friends by his straightforward way of begging, "I want a hundred dollars from you," but the amount secured this way wasn't enough to keep his head above water. The dismal prospect of having to give up his good works saddened Father Tim's big heart. Providentially the word got around that he was hard up. Soon a group of prominent men interested a number of people in contributing a hundred dollars a year for three years to support the institutions. A load was lifted from Father Tim's mind.

Conciliatory work absorbed a good deal of his time and attention in 1915 and 1916. In December, 1915, he prevented a strike of drivers for express companies by persuading the express owners to raise salaries. With the help of the Rev. John J. Thompson he put an end to a one-week strike at the Fairbanks Soap Company. The workers got a raise. During this same month, February, 1916, he began to work on the strike at the American Stove Company.

The plant, located at King's Highway and Daggett Avenue, was run on the open-shop plan, employing about half union men and half nonunion. In February a few men struck because the company refused to collect the dues of certain delinquent union men. By March 3 over two hundred tinners, polishers, and mounters were involved. Father Dempsey urged them to get back to work for the sake of their families. Then he arranged a conference with the general manager, Mr. Louis Stockstrom, and four union leaders, headed by Mr. W. L. Funderburk of Detroit, general president of the Stove Mounters' Union of America. As a result of their meeting in Father Tim's presence on March 6, the union men finally agreed that their own organization should take care of the collection of dues, and the management of the plant agreed to restore to their jobs immediately all the tinners and polishers and to take back the mounters as soon as places opened up.

Strikes by the baggagemen and by workers at the Quick Meal Company and the Hydraulic Press Brick Company were settled with comparative ease, but the strike of 3500 members of twenty-one unions affiliated with the Building Trades Council made Father Tim weary and worried.

On May 1 about 500 skilled workmen, members of unions affiliated with the Building Trades Council, tied up the building industry in St. Louis when they struck in sympathy with the International Hodcarriers', Builders', and Common Laborers' Union, Local Number 22, whose demand for recognition, thirty-five cents an hour, and an eight-hour day had been refused by the Master Builders' Association. Labor leaders visited the various buildings in process of construction: Wagner Electric, Pevely Dairy, Busch, Sulzer Brothers Diesel Engine Company, Luyties Building, Fulton Iron Works, Orpheum Theater, and the *Post-Dispatch.* The workmen left their jobs quietly and without disturbance.

That very day Father Tim arranged a conference between a representative of the Fruin-Colnon Construction Company and Mr. Charles J. Lammert, president of the Building Trades Council. His word of warning was, "You men are starting something that you can't stop if the brakes aren't put on at once."

But the brakes were not put on. The strike gained momentum. In two weeks 3500 members of twenty-one unions were taking an expensive vacation and construction was practically at a standstill. Trade and industry were suffering; the lot of many families was hard. Both parties to the controversy were anxious to smooth affairs out, but neither would take the first step. By May 15 both sides were thinking of compromise, but who would bring them together?

Father Dempsey arranged for a meeting of the representatives of the rival groups at the Century Building that afternoon. When he arrived, he could sense a spirit of hostility between the two groups, despite their anxiety to end the strike. Lammert, representing the union men, offered a compromise in which he demanded thirty-one and one fourth cents an hour, recognition of the Laborers' Union, and time and one half for overtime with double time for Sunday. After a brief consultation the Master Builders' committee refused the offer.

The air was tense. Lammert looked at Maurice Cassidy, secretary of the Council, and Steve McCoy, business agent for the Laborers. They got the message. The three of them got up and headed for the elevator, shouting, "It will be a war to the end."

Before the door of the conference chamber was shut, Father Dempsey was on his feet. He ran to the door and shouted at the departing group, "Here you, Cassidy! Keep your men out there till you hear from me; this isn't over yet."

While the union men cooled their heels and their tempers down the hall, Father Tim argued with the representatives of the Master Builders' Association. Finally they made an offer which Father Tim thought might satisfy the union men. He called them back into the conference room. They listened to the offer: thirty cents an hour for building laborers and carpenters' helpers, a maximum working day of nine hours, time and a half for overtime and double time for Sundays and holidays; nonrecognition of the Laborers' Union, and refusal to be bound by scale for excavators and wreckers

Father Dempsey's First Hotel for Workingmen.

The new quarters of the Hotel for Workingmen provided a decent home for men who wanted to be decent.

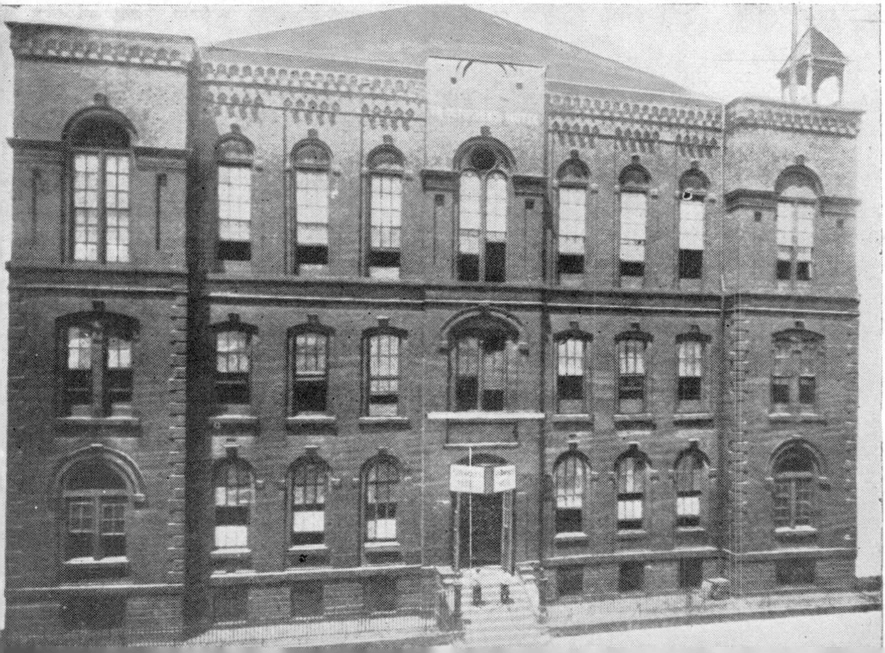

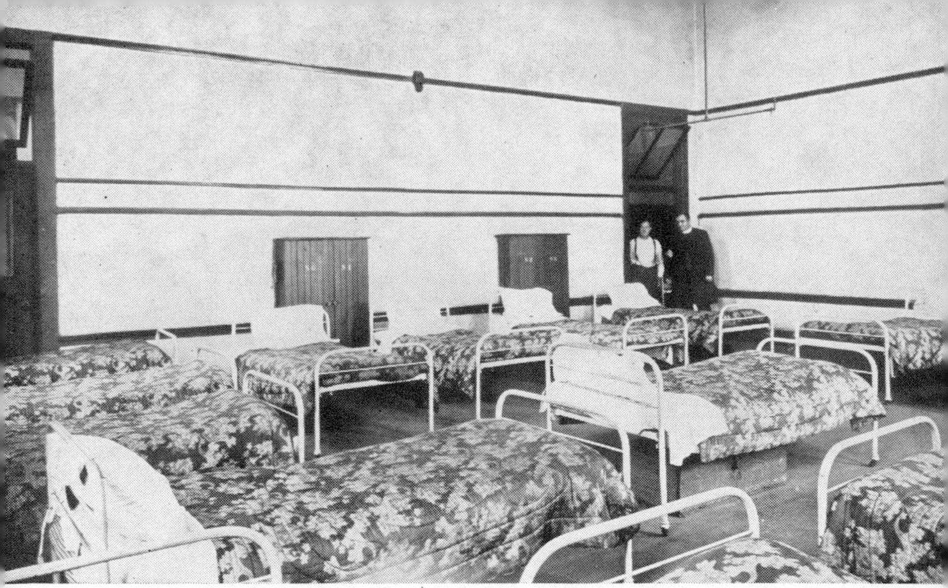

The dormitories in the Hotel for Workingmen were clean and friendly because "men were not born to roam without a fixed abode."

The recreation room in the Workingmen's Hotel was the scene of numerous entertainments, meetings, and informal gatherings.

The Hotel at Broadway and Dickson Street was an effort to create a homelike atmosphere.

Company A of Father Tim's Club for Workingmen paraded in October 1908 for the cornerstone laying of the St. Louis Cathedral.

Greeting an old friend and dinner guest at the Men's Hotel was an act of genuine courtesy springing from true love for men.

Father Tim becomes Monsignor Timothy Dempsey.

The new Hotel for Workingwomen on Hogan Street was palatial in the estimation of hundreds of women who there found comfort and protection.

The Irish Pipers and the famous bus before Father Tim's rectory.

Presentation of $36,000 fund raised by St. Louis citizens and presented to Father Tim for his charities.

In the long lines, Father Tim (facing the camera) could single out professional and businessmen and laborers whose stooped shoulders told the story of the depression.

Father Tim was always an interesting and convincing speaker.

During his funeral thousands of all ages and conditions of life stood outside the church in the bright morning sun.

First Holy Communion at St. Patrick's was an opportunity for Father Tim to express his interest in the colored members of his flock.

Father Tim's final resting place is under a celtic cross in Exiles' Rest.

ST. LOUIS STAR-TIMES

"FATHER TIM."

An important position is open at Sixth and Biddle streets in St. Louis. The pay, as far as money goes, is small, but there is other remuneration compared with which the salary and bonus of the highest-paid business executive in the United States is a mere stipend. Love and respect from the poor, the downtrodden, the underprivileged and the material failures in life's battle; consciousness of doing God's work for the sake only of doing good; knowledge that, when the task is finally laid down, an entire city will mourn the passing of something great and fine—these are some of the extra emoluments.

Father Tim—the Right Reverend Monsignor Timothy Dempsey, to quote his full title—pastor of St. Patrick's Church in what some people call the slums, has suddenly died. He had all the fine qualities that so many priests of his church possess, but in larger degree than many of them. He had, besides, certain attributes that are rare among the best of men anywhere, in any walk of life. His homes for the working poor were not unusual in large cities. Neither was his church, nor the places where men were fed when they had been denied food everywhere else. It was the combination of these efforts, and the broad charity and understanding with which Father Tim administered them, that were unusual. He could be fair to employers, as to employes, when labor chose him as an arbitrator in its troubles. He knew that relief problems in time of distress cannot always be judged by the cold rules of social economics. He never forgot that, after all, men are men.

Someone else, of course, will succeed him as pastor and carry on Father Tim's work. The task cannot be abandoned. Centuries hence, perhaps, authorities of his church, digging into the remote past, will decide that in St. Louis, in the year 1936, there lived and died a priest who had all the qualities of a saint. If the records are searched carefully enough, it will be found that Father Tim's contemporaries already had conferred on him that title unofficially.

St. Louis Globe-Democrat.

TUESDAY, APRIL 7, 1936.

The Globe-Democrat is an independent newspaper printing the news impartially, supporting what it believes to be right and opposing what it believes to be wrong without regard to party politics.

FATHER TIM.

In the Catholic hierarchy he was enrolled as Monsignor Timothy Dempsey, but among those whose lives he touched intimately with the satisfying benediction of practical charity, and among those who, more fortunate in worldly estate, learned to love him for his deeds of good, he was known as Father Tim. It was a name he liked. No elevation of rank within his church could wean him from his place among the humble, from his labor in the Lord's vineyard in the capacity not only of priest, but also as friend to all men. His was a universal charity, a philanthropy that countenanced no barriers of race, creed or previous wrongdoing. He answered far better than most of us the question from the Scripture: "Am I my brother's keeper?" He distinctly felt that he was when his brother needed assistance.

During his 39 years as pastor of St. Patrick's Church, he became one of the best known St. Louisans, probably the best. Mention has been made of his charities, such as his hotels for working men and women, his day nursery, his food kitchen, which fed thousands without questions asked. But vast and important as were these achievements, he attained high status in another sphere. For many years when labor was in dispute with employers, the disagreeing parties almost automatically turned to Father Tim as the final arbiter. Many hours he spent at shirt-sleeved conferences with them. He talked their language and he minced no words—but his methods got results.

His parish was located in a section of the city where the extra-curricular activities he followed were frequently necessary. Gangsters, bootleggers, thieves—he knew them and their derelictions. He laid a heavy hand on them for their sins, but if there came the time of death-bed repentence, he spoke words of consolation and hope. His "Pax vobiscum" has launched many such prodigals into eternity.

But aside from this practical application of the brotherhood of man, Father Tim's niche in the affections of this city is due to his unostentatious portrayal of tolerance in all things, including religion. That is why his intimate friends, the generous donors to his various projects, included as many Protestants and Jews as Catholics. They were attracted by the robust sincerity of the man, by his scorn for what we may call social reform against a background of science, by his belief that if a man or woman is in want, such an individual must be helped immediately with food and shelter. Let the good advice come later. "Religion and an empty stomach don't mix," he used to say. In his daily chore of helping everyone who called at his door regardless of who they were, he preached unwittingly powerful sermons on tolerance and contributed largely toward the enviable reputation St. Louis holds in this respect.

Father Tim literally worked himself to death. Long ill, he drove himself at his manifold tasks until he broke under the strain. "He overworked his heart for the poor," said Archbishop Glennon. But Father Tim did not think of being overworked. "He seemed to think he would live forever," said his sister.

So he will. Father Tim's memory will be revered so long as men may speak of the good he did. His grave in "Exile's Rest," a plot in Calvary, where he will rest beside a hundred of his "boys," will be a shrine for years to come. The poor have lost a constant, understanding friend. The city has lost a splendid man, whose mission of mercy and kindness carried him far outside the orbit of his priesthood.

Two of the editorials which appeared after Father Tim's death.

since builders were not able to bind their subcontractors. Cassidy said bluntly, "We'll submit it to the committee."

At eleven o'clock on Tuesday morning, May 16, the executive committee of the Building Trades Council accepted the compromise offer of the Master Builders' Association. The strike was over. Men would be back at work; trade and industry would go on; families would eat again; the construction of the new buildings would advance. Father Tim was happy. In an interview he expressed a conviction born of Gaelic optimism, "I believe this will be the end of strikes in St. Louis."

The newspapers, as usual, attributed the settling of this strike to the timely intervention of Father Tim. Many people were calling him the greatest living Missourian. In a letter to the editor of the *Post-Dispatch* one reader said: "The Governor need not look far to find the State's greatest living citizen. He lives in St. Louis and will be revered as a saint when the political colonels and so-called statesmen will have been long forgotten. . . . Hand the honor to Father Timothy Dempsey without further ado." But Father Dempsey was not looking for awards and honors; he had come "to minister, not to be ministered to." There would be enough celebrating and honoring when his silver jubilee of ordination to the priesthood came in June.

Chapter 8

A PRIEST FOREVER

FATHER DEMPSEY'S realization of the privileges, responsibilities, and dignity of the priesthood had deepened with the passage of years. Priests in good or bad standing always received a reverential welcome at St. Patrick's rectory. The third floor of the house was open to them. Even a man who for long years disgraced the priesthood could count on a friendly reception at Father Tim's. He helped poor students for the priesthood by lodging them during the summer and by paying for their training in the seminary. The priesthood in his mind was not a mere profession; it was a sublime vocation. The priest was *Soggarth Aroon,* "priest of my heart."

In a sermon delivered on the occasion of the Rev. John Lonergan's first Mass, offered at St. Patrick's on June 9, 1911, Father Dempsey gave eloquent expression to his ideas on the priesthood. "Nothing that man has ever done, nothing that man could ever do, could possibly be greater than the consecration of the Body and Blood of Christ, and therefore no position that man may occupy or aspire to, more exalted than that of God's priest. Worldly honors and worldly positions are like the flowers that bloom for a while but are doomed to wither and die. Kings and rulers will pass away; kingdoms will rise up and flourish and fade, but there is one the solidity and endurance of whose strength and stability are communicated from the rock upon which Christ built His Church, and this one is the Priest Forever according to the order of Melchisedech. The priest by ordination partakes of the priesthood of Christ, the great High Priest."

With sympathetic understanding he traced the story of a priest's training: "The priest must not seek happiness in worldly things. His source of joy is in God's sanctuary; his thoughts and aspirations for the glory of God; his zeal for the increase and extension of God's kingdom. Of him especially must be true the words of our Lord, 'He that loveth father and mother more than Me is not worthy of Me.'

"Hence the Church exhorts her priests in fostering vocations to take the boy before worldly thoughts have captured his mind, bring him under the influence of religious education in the preparatory seminary where she has her teachers to lead him step by step through the fundamental paths to the more extensive fields of philosophy and theology. There he learns under trained masters the great truths which it is his mission to teach, for he is to be one with Christ, to teach the world to observe Christ's truths. He is to judge the world in the tribunal of penance, to offer with Christ day by day the sacred Body and Blood for the sins of the world.

"And as the young man urged on by the spirit of his sublime vocation realizes more and more, year by year, the awful obligations which the priesthood entails, and when fear might make him shrink from assuming such serious responsibilities, the influence that such fear might exercise is counteracted by the thought that he is called by God, that He who said, 'My yoke is sweet,' will sustain him; that he is privileged beyond the angels in being entrusted with the power of calling down on the altar the Son of God. Hence, casting aside fear, he longs for the day when with the imposition of the Bishop's hands he receives the power which gives him the privilege of calling his friends together to rejoice with him in his great joy, on the day of his first Holy Mass."

Rising to new heights of eloquence, Father Tim in his pleasing brogue interpreted the sentiments of the young priest, the Church, and the priest's parents: "Yes, a day like this brings many reasons for joy and happiness. It is one of surpassing joy to the young priest, the realization of all his sacred thoughts and aspirations; to be permitted to ascend to God's altar, to raise the consecrated hands above his friends in blessing, to pray for the loved ones, living and dead, and grander than all, to pronounce the solemn words which change the material substance of the bread and wine into the Body and Blood of Christ. It is a day of joy for God's Church who entrusts to her priests the deposit of faith to be preserved and proclaimed to the world. What a joy for her, the pure spouse of Jesus Christ, as she sees the soul without guile become the resting place of the Holy One whose desire is to be with the children of men. And what words can express, this morning, the sentiments of those to whom the young priest was given by Almighty God to be brought up in His fear and love!"

Five years had passed since he delivered this sermon at Father Lonergan's first Mass. It was time to celebrate his own Silver Jubilee as a priest. After calling attention to the anniversary in the *Hotel Magazine,* Michael Gallagher predicted that:

> Not merely in this city, amongst those who know and love him, will the occasion be honored by kindly remembrance and good will, but wherever a group of toiling men exchange experiences of their wanderings and their hardships, when the job was far to seek, or the snow had seeped into the paper soles, when the note of defiance to an adverse fate that once sounded so heroic was gone, they will remember Father Dempsey's as a station of relief and haven of hope. . . . Neither brass nor monumental marble shall outlast his work.

The daily press, which announced even Father Dempsey's birthday year after year, gave a great deal of space to the jubilee celebration. After making the rounds of his institutions, Father Tim visited a Greek barber on North Broadway for a shave.

When he got back to Sixth and Biddle, he took his accustomed place in front of the church to greet the people as they arrived for the jubilee Mass. He knew practically all of them by name. If he didn't know a name, he would boldly yet inoffensively ask the name of the person.

Father Tim was celebrant of the Mass, the Rev. Francis Gilfillan, deacon, the Rev. John Godfrey, subdeacon, the Rev. M. S. Brennan and the Rev. Maurice O'Flaherty, masters of ceremony, and the Rev. D. J. Lavery, preacher. The organist and choir surpassed themselves in their effort to make the occasion memorable. Father Tim was quite exhausted when the Mass ended at 11:45.

At the banquet and reception the Rev. P. P. Crane of St. Lawrence O'Toole's parish, later vicar-general and pastor of Holy Name parish, presented a purse of $2,200 from the priests, Mr. William J. Kinsella a gift of $3,200 from the laity, the graduating class of St. Patrick's a small money gift with a letter of congratulations, and the newspapermen a generous money gift along with a handful of compliments.

Father Crane's presentation address brought the red to Father Tim's cheeks. "During these twenty-five years that have whitened your hair to the silver of their number, you have always been a priest of the people, for the people, and by the people. You have lived among them; you have shared their joys and sorrows as only a priest may. Out of this nearness to the people has come your knowledge of their needs, and from this knowledge have come your renowned institutions that are known from the Atlantic waters where stands the statue of Liberty to the Golden Gate of the Pacific and from the winter winds of the northland to the Savannas of the South. In fact, your name and hotels are world known. . . . You have had, and you have compassion on the multitudes. God made you large in body to give full play to the big heart within you throbbing with love for humanity.

"You are indeed a social worker without fads or fancies. No dreamer you. Yours is not 'an organized charity, scrimped and iced, in the name of a cautious, statistical Christ,' but working out concretely and in daily life the Catholic doctrine of the Brotherhood of Man in the Fatherhood of God. Your left hand knows not what your right hand gives. . . .

"Where are all my thoughts – inspired by your life – leading me but to a recognition of the place of the Catholic Church in the social order; that the world's weariness must find rest in her bosom; that the restoration of all things in Christ must come through her. . . .

"May the Blessed Christ whom you serve in the poor be your abiding strength toward many a day before it be the evening time to hallow your end with the golden glow of a Golden Jubilee. And then an afterglow. At your going out may the many weary ones who found earthly and heavenly rest through you be the noble company that shall meet you – an exile too – to take you home. God keep you, Father Tim."

Father Crane was scarcely finished before the newspapermen had their say. Father Tim had always maintained friendly relations with the members of the newspaper fraternity. He was good "copy" for them because of his unique personality and his public importance. They in turn did him the favor of freely and copiously advertising the needs of his various institutions. Even when a scribe put in Father Tim's mouth words which he never used, such as "Begorrah" and "Bedad," he would merely laugh and say of the reporter, "Isn't he a lad. Wait until I catch him."

One of the drinking members of the fraternity always called at the rectory when he was on a spree. Father Tim would answer the doorbell himself and say, "That I may never sin or do harm, if it isn't. . . . Come in." They would have a long talk. Then for two or three days the spreeing newspaperman would follow Father Tim around like a pet poodle, up and down the stairs and to the door and telephone. After that he would disappear until the next spree. Father Tim felt sorry for the man. "It's a pity," he said, shaking his head, "he's such a brilliant fellow."

Father Dempsey often commented on how generously the newspapers treated him and his work for the Church. When he turned in his annual report one time, he said quite simply, "The newspapers are entirely responsible for our success." But on this jubilee day the newspapermen were going to let Father Tim know how they felt about him.

Their representative, Mr. Bernard Gruenstein, read a letter signed by the majority of prominent newspapermen in town.

Dear Father Tim:

We, the undersigned, reflect several creeds, and no creeds in particular, but on this occasion of your Silver Jubilee we are united in one creed: We believe you are a grand old scout.

We know and admire you for your sterling merit, your simple devotion to the poor and weak, your chivalrous championship of the underdog.

No plumed knight in days of old ever battled more bravely for the hand of the fair than you have done for the down-and-out of St. Louis. Your plumes are not gay feathers cruelly plucked from the wings of helpless fowls; your plumes are human souls struggling to get on their feet, and these you wear about your big Irish heart with a grace excelling that of any cavalier on any cloth of gold.

Not satisfied with this laudation which almost embarrassed good Father Tim to death, the newspapermen had Mr. Gruenstein read some congratulatory verse composed by one of their number for the occasion. It recounted once more the Father's good deeds and happily concluded with the lines:

And so we come of every creed,
Of every tongue and race,
On this your Silver Jubilee
The story to retrace.

A wish we'd make, good Father Tim —
And may the silv'ry light
Turn softly on your path to gold,
And shine beyond the night.

Father Tim loved these lads from the papers, and in his acceptance talk he told them so, just as he had told the priests, the laity, and the graduating class. They were right about his devotion to the poor, the weak, and the underdog.

To these he had consecrated his life. When someone asked him whether he would choose a richer parish if he had the choice to make again, he said, "No, I know these people and this is the best place for me."

Father Tim realized that numbers of the working class had left the Church because the Christian world had, in the words of Jacques Maritain, left the working class. The strength of socialists and communists came less from their ideology than from the fact that they lived with the masses; in fact, they bound themselves to the masses. Father Tim was applying the papal social doctrine by living with the masses, by binding himself to them. He was rarely away from the parish. There were a few journeys to Ireland, necessitated by the condition of his health, and there were single trips to Chicago, New York, and Washington on necessary business. Yes, he was a priest of the people, for the people, and by the people.

This same idea was expressed by the Apostolic Delegate, Monsignor John Bonzano, in his congratulatory message: ". . . judging from the fruit of your labors, your years in the priesthood have been so wonderfully spent in the interest of God's poor and forsaken children that I think you may with modest proportion repeat of yourself those beautiful words of Christ, *Evangelizare pauperibus misit me.* Your greatest happiness and consolation on the day of your anniversary will be, I am sure, to recall to mind all the good that it has pleased God to accomplish through your instrumentality."

Praise is a strong wine that goes to many people's heads. It is more difficult for most men to carry praise gracefully than to carry their liquor. If Father Tim had not been solidly grounded in the sense of dependence on God, he might have lost his balance in the gale of compliments and honors that blew his way. But he asked himself the scriptural question, "What have we which we have not received; and if we have received, why do we glory as if we had not received?" Then, too, he looked upon the celebration as his friends' way of honoring the priesthood rather than honoring him as an individual priest.

When night fell, Father Tim was glad to lay his tired head on the pillow with a fervent "Glory be to God." Tired as he was, his thoughts may have turned to his own ordination at St. Patrick's College, Carlow. He was proud of the fact that he was a Carlow man. It was the first college established in Ireland after the penal laws had been relaxed. It produced the Most Rev. Dr. Doyle who gained emancipation under Daniel O'Connell in 1829; Dr. William P. Cahill, the renowned orator and lecturer; the first cardinal of Ireland, Cardinal Callen; and the first cardinal of Australia, Cardinal Moran. It gave to the United States two of its most accomplished pulpit orators: Bishop England of Charleston and Bishop Ryan of St. Louis and Philadelphia. Yes, he was fortunate in being a Carlow man. Twenty-five years ago, June 14, 1891, when he was only twenty-four years old, the ordaining bishop had made him a priest forever. Yes, a priest forever. The sacred character of the priesthood could not be blotted out. He was God's man, and henceforth it would be his vocation:

> To live in the midst of the world without wishing its pleasures;
> to be a member of each family, yet belonging to none;
> to share all sufferings;
> to penetrate all secrets;
> to heal all wounds;
> to go from men to God and offer Him their prayers;
> to return from God to men to bring pardon and hope;
> to have a heart of fire for charity,
> and a heart of bronze for chastity;
> to teach and to pardon, console and bless always.

Now, after twenty-five years of sacerdotal life Father Tim could appreciate the penetrating insight shown by Lacordaire in his estimate of the priesthood. The good priest's life was a rigorous one, but it had its consolations. His thoughts flew back two years to the time of the terrible fire at the Missouri

Athletic Club with its holocaust of thirty-nine persons. It hadn't been easy for him to plunge into those devouring flames to hear the confessions of three men pinned under the burning wreckage. He had come out bleeding, scorched, and almost naked, but he was happy, for the men would soon be with God. The grace of God made it possible to accept graciously the rigors of his life. It would not be lacking during the years that stretched before him. How many years? That was up to God. There would always be problems enough to engage his busy mind and arouse his heart to action.

Chapter 9

SPREADING OUT

A FIRE at the nursery, which caused more excitement than damage, emphasized the need for new and safer quarters. With the somewhat sporadic backing of various St. Louis groups, including a Board of Lady Managers, an addition to the parish school building, containing nineteen rooms and two outdoor sleeping porches and costing $12,000 and plenty of worry for Father Tim, was finally built in 1912.

Archbishop Glennon, members of fashionable families, and hundreds of poor people were present for the grand and formal opening on October 12, Columbus Day. After blessing the building, the archbishop expressed a hope that the debt would be paid off quickly. "Babies are very sensitive creatures," he said, "and do not like to be in a mortgaged building. This charity is an appealing one. People on the winning side are too apt to forget little abandoned children on the losing side. Perhaps Providence makes the child helpless so as to bring out the humanity that is in us and teach us not to struggle for ourselves, but for others. . . . May the fall season prove for Father Dempsey a spring-time of charity." Declaring that both the Workingmen's Hotel and the Working Women's Hotel had started without a cent and were soon out of debt, Father Tim in his answering talk promised that the nursery would quickly be out of debt also. He did not foresee the complications arising from the World War.

Like the children of the nursery, the women at the hotel needed more room. But they would have to wait; the world was at war. Father Dempsey's peace-loving heart was sad as he watched nation after nation succumb to the sucking maelstrom of war. Would circumstances finally force his adopted and beloved country to fight? Could the United States maintain the neutrality that President Wilson professed? Father Tim hoped so. He often said he hated war and words of war.

The prospect of the United States entering on the side of Great Britain was as repugnant to him as the singing of "God Save the King" on St. Patrick's Day. "Ireland must be free" was the slogan that burned itself into Father Tim's mind. He could sing and recite all the rebel songs and ballads. His strongly emotional nature entered deeply into the sentiments of these songs and ballads. The priest who could deal so charitably with individual Englishmen had no use for England and said so quite frankly. The England he had in mind was the England that tried by foul means to wrest the faith from the Irish, that impoverished and deliberately took away from them the means of education and then mocked the Irish for being poor and ignorant.

His frank, public declarations on this subject during the period when the United States government was trying to keep the ship of state on its course of neutrality had so much influence on popular thinking and on diplomatic relations that he was finally ordered by the government to keep silent. Strained relations between the United States and Germany culminated in a declaration of war on Good Friday, April 6, 1917. The nation set itself to the complicated process of wartime production and wartime living; Father Tim tried to reconcile himself to the will of God. But his natural feelings continued to foment revolution in the kingdom of his soul. The first World War was a hard blow for him. Only his intense love for the land that had adopted him and millions of Irishmen before him and the superabundant grace of God gave him the power to reconcile himself to the turn of events. He loved America. After Ireland the land of his adoption had the warmest spot in his heart.

From a bloody rostrum war taught the American people the hard lessons of cooperation and sacrifice. With tears in their eyes mothers and fathers waved a proud good-by to stalwart sons in khaki and in blue consecrated to the work of winning "the peace without victory" and "making the world safe for democracy." Those who kept "the home fires burning" began to learn that "priorities" was more than a difficult word to pronounce. They made their clothes last another season; they repaired articles that were formerly tossed away; they began to realize that coffee, sugar, and other eatables were blessings, not to be taken for granted, as the rationing system began to pinch. Liberty loans caused Uncle Sam's nephews and nieces to dig into their pockets; wars cost money, said Uncle Sam. A new thing called selective service hurried members of the family off to training camps. Father Dempsey watched the parade of events and prayed for an early peace according to the principles of Pope Benedict XV. He went on with his own little work of bringing peace to the hearts of those people who wandered into his life.

A nervous, exhausted world welcomed the collapse of the Central Powers in the fall of 1918. Factory whistles blew, church bells rang, men and women shouted or wept when the news of the November eleventh armistice flashed around the world. The war was over, thank God, the war was over. Those were Father Tim's sentiments, too. He was free now to turn his attention to the completion of the negotiations for acquiring the old St. Vincent Orphanage on Hogan Street for the use of his guests at the Women's Hotel.

In September the Daughters of Charity had transferred themselves and their charges from the old three-storied red brick structure on Hogan to a new and magnificent building in the St. Louis suburb of Normandy. This was Father Tim's chance. He would try to buy the building on Hogan Street. After the transfer of his guests and their residence at the old orphanage for a year under rental terms, Father Tim paid his first one thousand dollars on the $20,000 purchase price.

Not satisfied with the arrangements of the building, he determined to make extensive alterations up to $10,000. For three months carpenters, plumbers, electricians, and plasterers made themselves a temporary nuisance to Father Tim's guests, but when the workers had cleaned up the piles of old plaster, pieces of wire, rusty pipe, and heaps of sawdust and moved off to other labors, the women were glad to have put up with the discomfiture. Their new home was palatial.

On the day of formal opening, March 23, 1920, Father Tim told his 200 guests, "There are to be no rules and regulations about your coming and going. We expect every girl to be self-respecting and able to regulate her own conduct. There will be no singing or psalming in the Working Girls' Home." Gentle Mary Coughlin, whose motherly qualities had endeared her to the guests at the hotel on Broadway and Dickson, perpetuated the homelike spirit of the old institution as matron of the new. The hotel restaurant, offering meals at from 5 to 25 cents, would, according to Father Tim, serve "the keenest appetites and the slenderest purses." Of course, those whose purses were utterly flat would not be refused. The dollar to a dollar and a half charged for the rent of a room would serve to keep a woman's self-respect if not to meet the expenses incurred in the hotel's upkeep.

Operating expenses for all the institutions continued to run high for some time after the war. During the war Father Tim, to his utter disgust, had been forced by the high prices of articles to boost the rates at his Men's Hotel from ten cents to fifteen cents a day. He felt bad about that.

The Nursery and Emergency Home, which was always making his gray hairs white on account of financial worries, continued to be a losing proposition from the money angle. Baby powder and soap could not be dug in the backyard; bed linens and diapers did not grow on the few gasping hard maples in the St. Patrick's industrial district. And even nursery youngsters have to eat. If a Jewish friend, Berthold Price, had not come to Father Tim's assistance with generous money gifts, it is highly probable that the $12,000 investment would no longer have echoed the giggles, bawling, and shouting of carefree children.

The abortive efforts at securing a just and equitable international peace after four years of blood-letting provided Father Dempsey with some distraction from the burdens of his parochial work but afforded him little consolation. He had hoped to see the incorporation of the ideals and principles of Pope Benedict XV in the treaties. Instead he perceived that seeds were being sown for future wars. The persistent agitation of the "drys" in behalf of a prohibition amendment invited his frankly torrid criticism. He knew the futility of trying to legislate men into temperance. He predicted the bad effects of such an amendment, and when it actually took effect in January, 1920, some of the bad effects began to manifest themselves in his own parish. "Bootlegging" became a profession and gang wars over liquor districts in big cities reproduced in miniature the horrors of the recently finished world conflict. Father Tim found himself up to his neck in the troubled affairs of gangmen.

He watched, too, with a good deal of concern the efforts of a vociferous and determined minority of women to secure equal political rights with men. Along with many other thinking men whose respect for women was deep and whose conviction of the essentially different functions of men and women in a state was firm and enlightened, Father Dempsey with a certain prophetic insight bemoaned the funeral of chivalry in the adoption of the 19th amendment in August, 1920.

Yes, women would have equal rights, not only at the polls, but in streetcars; they could hang by a strap while men sat; they could fight to get on after doing a man's work in a shop or office. The male element would push "equal rights" down the throats of the once gentler sex. Chivalry would be as dead as the latest victim of a gangland feud left riddled with bullets in the weed patch along some lonely road. It hurt Father Tim to see the "ladies," as he always referred to them, yield their queenly throne in the home; it hurt Father Tim to see men killing each other in gangland's feuds. His chance to be peacemaker came in the 1920's.

Chapter 10

"THE POOR MISGUIDED BOYS"

GROUPS of men, anxious to pick up easy money, had marked off the districts of the city for their liquor run. Invasion of a rival group's district invited swift retribution in the ghastly form of murder. Business was business, and there must be no "hornin' in." By October, 1921, storm clouds were gathering over St. Louis gangland. At the end of the month the storm unleashed its fury. Men whom Father Tim had known since they were, as he puts it, "knee high to a duck," began to settle their territorial disputes with guns.

Willie Egan was shot and carried to the hospital in a dying condition. Egan's eyes lit up as Father Dempsey approached the bed.

"Willie, you said you couldn't promise me to keep away from this shooting, and now look at you," said Father Tim almost crying himself. He was alone with Egan. He put his arm around him. "Who shot you, Willie?"

"I don't know."

"Now, Willie, remember, you're dyin'. It's no time for holdin' things back."

"Father, I don't know. A car full of men whizzed by—and they got me."

Father Tim knew that Egan was telling the truth. He heard the dying man's confession and gave him *Viaticum* and Extreme Unction, for Egan was a sorry man. In a little while the repentant leader of the Egan group was dead in Father Tim's arms.

In the next few months it became clear to Father Dempsey

that the Egans had laid the blame for Willie's murder on a rival gang known as the Hogans. The smoldering fires flamed forth in January, 1922. An abortive attempt was made on the life of Jim Hogan and a henchman named Goldfeder. The Egans under their new leader, Dinty Colbeck, characterized by Father Tim as "afraid of no man in shoe leather," were blamed for the attack. The future had the hue of blood. The police could not prevent the murders; perhaps Father Dempsey could. The sentiment among certain men in police circles was that gang killings resulted in good riddance of bad rubbish. Although Father Tim had the highest respect for policemen in general, he did not share this brutal sentiment.

He knew some of the men on both sides personally; others he knew only by reputation. None of them, according to him, actually lived in St. Patrick's parish. As he called various members of the gangs to the rectory for individual conferences during the next few months, he came to know them better and to get at the root of their grievances. Some of the men he styled "decent, likable fellows." Shaking his head sadly, he would repeat again and again, "The poor, misguided boys that do be killin' each other – and the fathers of them the decentest men that ever came to America. . . . And not a mean boy among them." Not everybody agreed with Father Dempsey's charitable verdict, but that didn't change his mind.

Asked about the origins of the Hogan-Egan feud, he ascribed the trouble to a natural propensity of some of the men for leadership, a morbid desire for notoriety, and the drink habit. This natural propensity for leadership, he said, "often leads to words and sometimes to blows even among the higher-ups of this world. Drink has aggravated the situation. The two greatest curses upon this nation are drink and prohibition. . . . Drink is largely responsible for the trouble between the Egans and the Hogans. It makes men tyrannical. I have known many men who were tyrannical when drunk, but who were fine gentlemen when sober." Although he felt his indebtedness to the newspapers for advertising his needs and although he more than once publicly acknowledged this debt, he criticized them at this time for investing the activities of the gangs with a certain dubious glamor and romance. Such a slant in the papers did the gangsters no good and did the rising generation positive harm. He didn't like it.

By June, 1922, Father Dempsey had interviewed thirty-four members of the two factions and exacted from each of them the solemn promise not to be killing one another. Because they respected the fearless pastor whose heart went out to anybody in trouble, most of them were glad to come alone or in little groups to talk the whole thing over. They didn't resent his forthright admonition that they had no right to be taking other men's lives and that their endless wars were a bad thing for themselves and for the community. When Father Tim had finished the series of conferences, he told a reporter, "I feel safe in predicting that there will be no more murders so far as these two crowds are concerned." The news of the truce brought a sigh of relief from the people of St. Louis.

But the feeling of relief was short lived. On September second Abe Goldfeder and Max Gordon were shot at the corner of Locust and Jefferson. Police declared that the gang war had been resumed. Father Tim denied it.

"I am convinced that Goldfeder is not one of the boys who have been having so much trouble and I do not believe this shooting has anything to do with the Hogan-Egan affair. The boys have been coming to me every week and telling me about the feud. It is all over. A few of them have been carrying guns but there has not been a killing since they promised to quit."

In February, 1923, there was no doubt that the gangs were definitely "at one another" again, despite their solemn promises to Father Tim. Jacob Mackler, lawyer for the Hogan clique, and "Little Red" Powers, a member of the Egan gang, were murdered. Saddened by their infidelity to their promises, Father Tim said he would have another "talk with the boys."

"In the meantime I hope the boys will ignore the loose talk that is going around in police circles about who is going to be 'bumped off' next, and that sort of thing. If there is anything that will stir up more trouble between the two gangs, it is the predictions being made by detectives." He could talk freely about detectives since his brother, Frank, was one.

"I am convinced that Mackler was killed because of a false rumor that Max Greenberg, who was said to have engineered the killing of Constable William T. Egan more than a year ago, was back in town. If the idle gossip would cease, I believe the feud would end. At any rate I'm going to give the boys another little talk and see what I can do with them. I am going to handle them with diplomacy."

While he was engaged in this delicate diplomatic mission, the twenty-fifth anniversary of his pastorship rolled around. Although his official appointment to St. Patrick's was dated July 11, 1898, Father Tim made the jubilee celebration coincide with St. Patrick's Day.

A few days before the jubilee a newspaperman reported his interview with Father Tim. "Interviewing Father Timothy Dempsey . . . has many of the aspects of interviewing an exceedingly industrious governor of a busy state or the manager of the complaint bureau of a department store. For Father Tim, as he is known to his congregation, is spiritual adviser, employment director, and domestic arbiter of his flock.

"Since he came to the parish, a tall, strapping young Irishman, many a starving family has been fed through his efforts, many a failure in life has been strengthened and sent on his way, and many an unrepentant spirit has felt the smashing blow of his big right hand. For Father Tim, though a clergyman, is by the same token an Irishman, and has been known to deal swift punishment to those of his flock who transgress the bounds of decency."

"Mind you," said Father Tim, waving a big index finger in front of the reporter's face, "I've been in this parish twenty-five years come St. Patrick's Day. And this is what you call a tough neighborhood. But in those years or in my whole life I've never met a mean man yet, Catholic or non-Catholic. They're all good, lovable boys."

Pulling his 240 pounds and 6 feet 4 inches from the big armchair and smoothing the folds from his shiny black coat, he led the reporter to the door. Outside in the street dirty children played. Standing on the corner a group of his "b'ys" from the hotel were talking. "It doesn't look so inviting to some eyes," he remarked, casting a glance up and down the street in habitual wariness for the small boys' rock fight, "but it's gotten to be home to me and while I'm alive I'll stay here. I am the happiest man in the world. I wouldn't change places with any man. I have been told the work is too hard here, and asked to move. I couldn't do it."

After the jubilee Mass celebrated in the presence of the archbishop and a packed church, an informal reception was held in the parlor of the old rectory. The dingy walls reverberated with peals of laughter and the air fairly sizzled in the exchange of brilliant and gay repartee. As usual, Father Tim's stories, told in a way that betrayed a genius at the art, stole the show. But former Judge Daniel G. Taylor, representing a committee of St. Louis citizens, was one up on Father Tim when he presented the surprised, almost breathless, pastor with a check of $7,000 in testimony of appreciation for his work among the poor of the parish and the city generally. When Father Tim recovered his breath, thanked his friends, and remarked that the money would almost take him out of debt, Mr. Taylor said, "I hope we will never see you out of debt, for that condition would rob you of one of your noblest characteristics." Father Tim saw the point and blushed.

When the excitement of the reception had subsided a bit, a reporter asked Father Dempsey what emotions he felt on his jubilee day. "Praise God," said he, " 'tis a great day for my people, 'tis a great day for my children. I receive these things in their name for 'tis their anniversary you are celebrating. Their sorrows are mine and their joys are mine. I am glad if they are happy today. If I am of service to my people, may God spare me to them."

No doubt that was the prayer of thousands of people on his jubilee day. For in the words of the reporter, Father Dempsey, "powerful in physique, candid in his dealings with everyone, with a keen understanding of human nature and an unfailing love of his fellow man . . . has endeared himself not only to his parishioners but to thousands of people throughout the city, Catholics and non-Catholics alike. . . . Father Dempsey has never seen a picture show or a baseball game. Not that he objects to either, he will tell you, but the inhabitants of St. Patrick's parish give him plenty of other things to occupy his attention."

That night as Father Tim started to ascend the well-worn stairs, he cast a weary but benevolent glance at the heaps of letters and telegrams that covered his big office desk. He yawned. They would have to wait till the morrow. But what a treasure faithful friends were; they were worth more than all the money in the world.

As he lay in bed trying to induce sleep, perhaps his thoughts turned on the gangs and their activities. They were never long out of his mind. He was worried about them. Would they quit shooting each other and terrorizing the people of St. Louis? Would they agree to a truce and keep their word? Would the papers quit throwing a halo of romance around the heads of the gangsters? Would they quit building up the leaders to the proportions of imitable heroes?

A truce seemed far away when the rival gangs, ten days after the jubilee, began to open fire on each other. Residents along Olive and Locust between Grand and Jefferson were startled out of their early morning sleep on March 27 as two carloads of gangsters raced down the street firing at each other. Shots shattered the windows of the Hudson-Frampton Motor Car Company at 33rd and Locust. His property loss prompted Mr. Frampton to send a long telegram of protest to Governor Hyde:

> At 2:45 a.m. Tuesday our place of business was shot up by gangsters who were engaged in a running fight in racing automobiles. Our two main plate glass windows were shattered, greatly hampering our facilities for displaying motor cars with a resultant loss to our firm.
>
> We protest against this condition, which not only permits gangsters to run down children on the streets and shoot up places of business, but which permits murders, bank and payroll robberies, and other crime to flourish.
>
> The crime wave and the war of gangsters certainly demands that stronger action be taken both by the State and City officials if St. Louisans are to have the police protection to which they are entitled.

The newspapers also quoted him as advocating that the citizens of St. Louis raise a fund of $100,000 to hire lawyers and private detectives to rid the community of gangsters if the police couldn't. No doubt the sentiments expressed in the telegram were shared by many St. Louisans. In fairness to the rival gangs it must be said that they usually knew their targets. Now and then, however, a bullet did stray.

Within the next few days Father Tim spoke strong words to his "poor, misguided b'ys." That his words had their effect was proved by the appearance in the papers on April 1 of pledges signed by the two rival leaders, Ed Hogan and Dinty Colbeck. They had agreed to a truce.

The truce was still inviolate on May 10, Ascension Thursday, when Father Dempsey was invested as Domestic Prelate of the Pope's Household with the title of "Right Rev. Monsignor." Long before the time for the services friends were filing into old St. Patrick's. They wanted to be present as he was officially honored by the head of the Church, Christ's vicar on earth. Even the rival Hogan and Egan gangs were represented. As customary, Father Tim was standing at the door, shaking hands and calling each person by name, his expansive smile, sparkling blue eyes, and expressive face saying even more than his busy tongue.

The mixed audience of Catholics and non-Catholics listened attentively to the reading of the official letter from Pope Pius XI:

> Your Archbishop has spoken of remarkable institutions of Christian charity established by you. For these as well as for the faithful fulfillment of your pastoral duties you are to be elevated, according to the rites of Holy Mother the Church, to the dignity of domestic prelate with the right to wear purple habiliments and in the Roman curia to put on validly and lawfully a linen shoulder garment with sleeves reaching to the hands, and the rochet, and at the same time to enjoy all honors, privileges, prerogatives and indults, which other ecclesiastics raised to this dignity do enjoy.

During the actual ceremony of investiture by the archbishop, Father Tim was bothered by a long Latin verb, *anathematizo,* meaning "I reject or damn." Finding the word too hard to pronounce, he substituted "And a Tim said so" wherever the word occurred in the rest of the liturgy. The archbishop with difficulty refrained from smiling.

In a short talk His Grace examined the social service methods of Monsignor Tim: "He is the best exemplar of sound social philosophy, namely, the helping of people to help themselves; but, if they cannot, then help them anyhow. I don't think our good monsignor has taken his philosophy out of books. I don't think he has paid much attention to bureaus or to surveys, but he has taken his philosophy out of his own great heart which beats in accord with the heart of Christ. In season and out of season, on the highways and in the alleys, he has been a force for righteousness. He has represented the blessed Christ who lived among the poor and lowly, making them His friends, His confidants, and finally His apostles."

Father Tim stirred uncomfortably during this episcopal eulogy. In his answering talk he thanked the archbishop for his constant aid and generosity and for the papal document. And in lighter vein:

"The finest boast that anyone can make is to be a friend of the Pope. This is a very bad neighborhood, here around St. Patrick's church, for anybody that is not a friend of the Pope, and it is going to be worse from now on because he had admitted me into his household. There are no bad people around here except those that stray in from the outside.

"I heard a priest the other night, referring to the great work done by the French pioneers, and after them by the Germans and the Irish, but he forgot to mention the Poles and Lithuanians, and the Slovaks, and the Italians, all of whom live in this neighborhood and are good people.

"My lines have fallen in goodly places," he continued as the congregation listened intently, "and it has been my privilege to work among those who follow the injunction of Almighty God, and earn their bread by the sweat of their own brow instead of somebody else's. I have often been asked how I could go on settling strikes. Well, I have never gone to see about a strike, when I didn't go first into this church, and kneel down by the altar and ask God to protect me, and ask St. Patrick's help also. Then I went over each time to the Day Nursery, and asked the Sisters to get the children to pray that the strike on which I was going might end for the benefit of the strikers, which it always did.

"The employers know my ways. I find out what the men who are working want, and as soon as that is determined, the rest is easy. There is more peace and contentment among the workingmen of St. Louis, and less radicalism, than in any city of the United States. The men who are leaders of the Building Trades Council, and the Central Trades and Labor Union, are all conservative workingmen. Once in a while they have labor troubles, but they don't last long."

A few months after his investiture as monsignor the gang wars were renewed. He had done his best to keep the warring factions at peace, but they had made the nest too hot for the dove of peace. It took years before the wars were curbed by the concerted and determined action of police, detectives, and post-office inspectors. Father Tim sadly watched the gangmen disappear one by one, either through shooting or through imprisonment. Not until the late 1920's would he again be engaged in the discouraging work of pacifying rival gangs, this time Sicilians.

Al Palazzolo was the reputed head of a gang which protected bootleggers against another gang known as the "Cuckoo gangsters" and extorted money from Italian businessmen. It was commonly known that this gang levied five cents on every bunch of bananas that came into St. Louis. The method of extortion was scientific. A member of the gang would enter Tony's fruit store and simply say, "We're getting up a purse for a sick family," or "Lend me fifty, Tony." Tony the fruit peddler knew better than to inquire about "the sick family" or to ask whether he would get his fifty back. Many small merchants had to give up their business because of the extortions of gangsters; others were forced into a condition of abject poverty. But in the late summer of 1927 the gangmen began to shoot each other up. Two factions of Sicilians were battling for supremacy in the field of extortion. Palazzolo was the leader of one gang; Tony Russo, the leader of the other.

Tony Russo and Vincent Spicuzza were brutally disposed of near Chicago on August 9. Benjamin Giamanco and a bystander, Aloys Beelman, were shot to death on August 24 between Pine and Chestnut Streets on Sixth. Al Palazzolo himself was riddled with bullets on September 9 at Tenth and Wash in the St. Patrick district. Charles Palmisano was pumped full of lead at Third and Franklin, and Frank and Salvadore Aiello were "bumped off" at Springfield, Ill., in early November. Charles Casamento was picked up bleeding and dying from bullet wounds in Carondelet Park on November 12. And the climax was reached on November 15 with the shooting of Ben Amato, owner of a bakery and oil station.

To Father Tim fell the lugubrious duty of burying some of these "misguided b'ys." After the service he would stand on the steps of the old church, shake his head sadly from side to side, and exclaim, "Too bad. They were once good boys. All my children, and we have to take care of them." He knew – and the knowledge grieved him – that the reason they wanted easy money, these gangsters, was to lead a wastrel's life.

The alarmed community of St. Louis naturally turned to Father Dempsey whose specialty was peacemaking. If anyone could do anything about curbing the shootings, it was he. On November 18 he told a reporter, "I will talk to the men whose names have been connected with the feud, and ask them, in the name of God and humanity, to stop hating and killing each other. I will point out to them that they are attracting criticism to their nationality. It is not my plan to gather them all together for one conference, but to have heart-to-heart conversations with them, one at a time."

So during the next few months he added to his regular duties the difficult task of interviewing men whose hearts were full of hate. Father Caesar Spigardi, pastor of St. Charles Borromeo church, helped him. The *Fascisti* of St. Louis, many other societies, and *Il Pensiero,* an Italian newspaper, all labored to turn public opinion so violently against the wars that they would be forced to cease. The police under chief Gerk and the detectives under chief Kaiser backed the propaganda methods with an unprecedented show of force. More police cars cruised around lower St. Louis and the danger spots, carrying men armed with submachine guns, automatic pistols, and revolvers.

All these elements together finally forced the Sicilian gangsters under cover, and the people of St. Louis breathed freely again. And Father Tim was free to give his energy and time to other important tasks.

Chapter 11

TIM SPEAKS HIS MIND — AS USUAL

EXCEPT when he was sick, Father Dempsey always had plenty of energy for active good works and he was as lavish with his time as a shrew is with her scoldings. But he did not always have the money he needed. During the year of the Sicilian gang wars a nonsectarian fund-raising committee was organized to give his many works a financial boost. Bennett Champ Clark, later United States Senator, was chairman. Other leaders were former Circuit Judge Samuel Rosenfeld, Pat Price, who had come to his rescue in 1917, George S. Johns, chief editorial writer for the *Post-Dispatch,* Isaac A. Hedges, Isaac F. Gradwohl the jeweler, and Arthur J. Fitzsimmons, prominent political figure. The leaders and their helpers strove to stir the collective conscience into giving more money to Father Dempsey's works.

One day Mr. Johns invited Father Tim to the committee's headquarters in the Federal Commerce Trust Building. He offered no explanation. Father Tim came. The office was somewhat crowded by the committee leaders and by newspaper reporters and photographers. He knew that something was up. Little Mr. Johns, a head shorter than the priest, gray headed with bald spots showing on the forehead and with a white mustache, walked up to him and looking him in the face said to him from the heart, "Father Tim, we all know you and love you. We know you have the strength of a giant, the gentleness of a woman, and the faith of a child. We are happy to be able to give this to you to carry on your good work." And he handed over a bank book with the remark that $36,-

000 had been deposited to Father Dempsey's account and presented another leather-bound book containing the lists of contributors to the fund, letters of praise, and clippings telling about the campaign.

After the handclapping had subsided, the newly endowed pastor told them how grateful he was. "You have made me independent. Many a time I've been in debt up to my neck and said nothing. I'll know how to use this; I won't carry it to my grave."

While the drinks and cigars were being passed around during the informal party, he regaled the men with stories. He asked them if they had heard of Dominic? "Well, Dominic was a terrible drinker. He finally quit when I got after him. And do you know, he saved $7,000 in ten years." Then he asked them whether he had told them about the Irish politician. "He was campaigning for parliament. In his talks to the voters he promised them that he'd marry the queen and paint all houses green. But he lost the election. That's gratitude, isn't it?"

With a $36,000 bank account Father Tim wouldn't have to worry so much about taking care of his newest foundation, a convalescent home in connection with the Women's Hotel. He had long wanted to provide a home for women who had been released from hospitals but were not yet strong enough to take up their regular duties. In November, 1924, the south wing of the hotel had been remodeled to accommodate about twenty-five patients. The fees were slight. For those who wanted to be independent a maximum of $6 a week was charged; convalescents of smaller means paid less; and those without any money – there were many of these – were never embarrassed. A physician and nurse called in case of need. He had justified this new venture by quoting from a classic of the spiritual life, *The Imitation of Christ,* in which the comment is found, "There is no standing still spiritually." "And this is true about things that are temporal, too," added Father Tim.

The burden of management fell largely to the capable hands

of the hotel matron, Mary Coughlin. But Father Tim, not the sort of man to relinquish authority easily, kept careful tab on the convalescent home as he did on the White Cross Crusade which he had inherited from the pastor of St. Leo's two years earlier (1922).

The purpose of this Crusade was to gather old papers, magazines, rags, furniture, and other discarded articles, sell these items, and then apply the revenue to the St. Patrick's institutions, especially the nursery. The general aim was to prevent tuberculosis among the poor, hence the name "White Cross." Employing about a hundred men and using seven trucks, the Crusade with central headquarters at 3525 Cozens Avenue was a busy organization. It helped pay the bills.

But life for Father Tim was not just a succession of worries about finances and concern about management of the institutions during these years. There were lighter moments. One such lighter moment was the priests' banquet in honor of the twenty-fifth anniversary of Archbishop Glennon's arrival in St. Louis (1928). Because of his reputation for a sparkling wit and skill as an after-dinner speaker, Father Tim was chosen to give the main speech. There was a clinking of glasses, a sliding of chairs, and a gradual expiration of conversation as he was introduced. Swallowing a glass of water, he stretched himself to his six feet four inches and began:

"It is a great honor, your Grace, to be selected from a body of over 600 priests to greet you on the completion of the 25th anniversary of your coming to us. We well remember the occasion of the conferring of the pallium in the Old Cathedral. I was then honored by being selected as cross-bearer. It was the only time your Grace ever made me carry a cross.

"The last time I addressed the clergy was when Francis Gilfillan was consecrated Bishop of St. Joseph. After the dinner was over, Father Wilbur remarked to some of the brethren that I made a great speech entirely. Someone replied that it was all right, but I didn't mean it! May the Lord have mercy on the dead!

"After the Eucharistic Congress in Chicago a stately figure of a man came up Sixth Street clad in purple cassock and feriola, and the biggest pectoral cross you ever saw. He rang the doorbell, and said he was Bishop of Montenegro and Patriarch of Serbia. 'You are the same to me, your Grace,' I said, 'as if you were Archbishop of Cork and Patriarch of all Ireland. Come in, your Grace, and if you stay long enough, you will see all your countrymen around here who hadn't sense enough to stay at home.' 'Ah,' said he, 'you speak like your Archbishop.'

"I was flattered. Of course, he told the truth, because nobody ever accused your Grace of making any distinction whether your devoted clients came from the banks of the Shannon, or the Rhine, or the Mississippi, or those countries that have no banks at all."

Then looking toward Monsignor Tannrath and Monsignor Crane, Father Tim got in a little personal dig.

"Of course, some of us fondly imagined we were better fitted to be the rector of the New Cathedral than Monsignor Tannrath, or better Vicar-Generals than Monsignor Crane; but, after all, we knew you meant those appointments for the best anyway." Their fellow clergy seemed to enjoy the discomfiture of the two Monsignors.

Father Tim then told about the founding of his Hotel for Men and referred to the $500 donation by the Archbishop. "That is the best thing you ever did in your life. We gave courage to the wayfarer not to seek shelter from the cold in places where he had to sing 'Nearer My God to Thee,' when he didn't mean it, or 'Land of the Pilgrim's Pride,' when he didn't mean it either. That reminds me of a man who used to visit the places where the Nordic blondes uplift the southern European barbarians. The woman missionary accosted Pat Welsh as he looked in the window of the mission. 'Brother,' she said, 'won't you come in and join the service?' 'No, ma'am, I don't want to go in,' said Pat. 'Ain't you a Christian?' she said. 'No,' he replied, 'I am an Irishman.'"

When the ripple of laughter had spent itself, Father Dempsey's face took on a more serious look as he continued. "The ringing tones of your voice have been an inspiration to us all. They are like the song of the thrush in the bushes around Old Clonard. No mocking bird notes are heard when you thrill your listeners in the New Cathedral. You don't descend to those petty discussions about the separation of Church and State, nor tell the Pope of Rome what you would do to him if he has any designs on America – nor do you call for the restriction of emigration.

"It's a pity that question of emigration didn't come up when the Indians owned this country. One of them said to me some time ago. 'You know we never had any luck since the Pilgrims landed on Plymouth Rock.' 'It's a pity,' I said, 'that the rock didn't land on the Pilgrims.' " It took a minute for the laughter to cease. . . .

"Nor do you talk about the workingmen's wages. 'Twas I did that when I gave the Carpenters' Union $1.10 an hour in May, 1923. Nor about feeding the hungry after the war. We all had a hand in that. I did my share and I didn't steal any German cows to do it either; and that's no Irish bull.

"We are all very fond of you today, your Grace, and wish and hope and pray 'that you may never die till the skin of a gooseberry makes a coffin for you.' "

The venerable Archbishop, who had endeared himself to his clergy and the people of St. Louis, in his answering talk countered with sparkling sallies of wit. Father Dempsey's talk was so well liked that the priests insisted on having it printed. It is one of the few talks by Father Tim still extant.

His reference to the carpenters' strike recalls his famous decision as arbitrator. A wage dispute had been going on between the Master Builders' Association and the Carpenters' District Council. Under pressure of the Association the carpenters had voted a 10 per cent reduction in wages, from $1.25 an hour to $1.12½. When the Association tried to enforce a 95c scale, Father Dempsey was called in as arbitrator. He fixed the wage at $1.10 an hour and made the following statement in connection with his decision:

"The assumption is not disputed that organization is necessary for the protection of the workers and the consequent well-being of society. Owners of capital in the most stable industries realize that their rewards are conditioned and safeguarded by the security assured to them through the unions against inferior output, both in quality and quantity. The experience and observation of your referee have shown him that the absence of cohesion amongst the unorganized masses destroys the sense of individual responsibility, which was so active during the war period when all labor was organized and busy.

"Welfare, like goodness, is self-diffusive. The satisfied employment of such a body of skilled men as the carpenters spreads its influence through all the circles of labor and business within the city and more remotely through the whole country.

"In reaching this award I was guided by the following: The carpenters require an expensive outfit of tools beyond all other mechanics, the purchase and maintenance of which must not be lost sight of in any equitable adjustment of wages. They have to be familiar with the general construction of a building in following the plans of the architect; in brief, their work is fundamental to the employment of other crafts, and to putting in motion the human and material resources that have been allowed to deteriorate too long." The Master Builders' Association had accepted the decision gracefully and the carpenters all rejoiced.

The archbishop's jubilee was a prelude to the fortieth anniversary of Father Dempsey's ordination to the priesthood, June, 1931. The newspapers as usual ran columns about the event. Father Tim expressed disappointment that Primo Carnera should have knocked out the Irish fighter Pat Redmond whose family home was near the Dempsey's in Ireland and whose father was born on the same day as Father Tim,

October 21, 1867. "If I had only been there!" he said clenching his fists while a mischievous smile played on his lips. He commented on a number of things for the benefit of the reporters, expressing his compassion for "children with legs like matches," condemning prohibition and the bootleg whiskey that "smells like hair-oil, turpentine, coal oil, everything but onions" and would "kill a dog," and telling about his hates and likes.

He indicated his warm disapproval of the terms, "prohibition," "camouflage," "propaganda," and "normalcy." As to the people he liked, he said, his eyes brightening:

"Now, take the nurses. How I do admire that class of people! Those beautiful young women, gifted, educated, fit to shine in any society, who give up their lives to relieve pain and suffering.

"And I like the newspaper people." One of his listeners cut in, "But, Monsignor, there's a Scotchman, Dr. Donald MacKenzie who says there ought to be a day of prayer for the press."

"There ought to be a week of prayer for the Scotch," snapped Father Tim with finality. Then he told them about the rich and the poor. "The poor especially are my friends, but the rich are pretty decent people. Some poor people speak bitter of the rich, and the dear Lord knows, maybe if we had the sorrows they have, we'd be bitter too. Last year it cost me about $70,000 to do the work I'm doing. Now the poor didn't give it to me, for they didn't have it. And I didn't pick any pockets. So it had to come from the rich. I wouldn't want to be rich myself. It's a great responsibility. But they can do good if they will."

During the next few months after the celebration he observed the sad effects of the world-wide depression in his district. Calls for food, clothing, fuel, medicine, and other necessaries were more frequent and more insistent. He saw the crowds of hungry, unemployed men multiply in St. Louis. He knew that 11,000,000 Americans were unemployed and that the nation was in a heart-searing agony of despondency. Relief stations began to appear in many cities. Bread lines became common. Father Tim determined to do his little bit to relieve the immediate necessities of the poor.

Chapter 12

"I WAS HUNGRY"

CERTAIN paradoxes about the depression puzzled Father Dempsey. One day as he walked out of the Mercantile Trust where he had just deposited money given to him by the late Hugh Campbell, he was cornered by newspaper reporters and asked to tell their readers about the paradoxes. Father Tim was glad to talk.

"What puzzles me, if these times be so hard as they say, is these long lines of people standing in front of the theaters downtown. Surely they're not all pickpockets. If times be so hard that everyone is hungry and out of a job, how are they buying tickets to a theater?

"Another thing that puzzles me, too, is how it comes they're yelling their heads off, watching the baseball game at Sportsman's Park – and it costs money to get in, and so many of them there that all the police in town are down at the field to see that they don't kill one another.

"Some of these men that are complainin' the most about depression are those that are getting $15,000 a year, to my knowledge, and a high-priced car thrown in. And such people, if you notice, are apt to say 'corr.' They can't stand up and say 'car' like an Irishman does who was trained in Dublin, where they speak the best English in all the world. No, they have to have their 'corr,' they do, and yet all the time be suffering a panic for fear they'll lose their meal ticket."

He stopped long enough to take a deep breath. "It is surely an odd world, a contradictory world. A socialist gave me $20 yesterday, knowing I belong to the I.W.W. I suppose he was afraid such a thing as money would burn a socialist's pocket. It wouldn't burn mine, I tell you."

It wasn't that Father Tim objected to the movies and baseball in themselves. On more than one occasion he had allowed friends and supporters of his institutions and of the Newsboys' Home of Father Peter J. Dunne to sponsor baseball games between major league stars for the benefit of these good works. One of the earliest night games in the history of baseball was played in 1909 between the St. Louis Browns and the Washington Senators for the benefit of Father Dempsey and Father Dunne. And on September 28, 1909, the St. Louis Cardinals battled the New York Giants in a benefit game at Kulage's Park under hundreds of arc lamps. No, he didn't object to innocent diversions, but he did object to a distorted sense of values. As to the theater people, the stage and movie actors and actresses, he entertained a friendly feeling for all the decent ones and welcomed them to the old rectory. Ed Wynn, for example, felt as much at home in old St. Patrick's as he did on the stage.

On his sixty-fourth birthday Father Tim dared to sing an optimistic tune in regard to the depression. He told the reporters: "We are on the last lap of the depression. I don't know it, I feel it, and that is the best way to know it. I want to be the first man to predict the glad news that after this winter we shan't have hard times any more for a while. The rich people are coming to the front for the help of the poor, and it is making a dent in the suffering. I believe that with the ending of this spell, as it is starting to end, things will be better than ever before."

When he was asked about his thirty-three years at St. Patrick's, he scratched his forehead in a characteristic gesture and observed, "Sure, and they've been years of trouble and grief – and a lot to be thankful for."

Someone then popped the India question and mentioned Gandhi. "Now, there's a lot of shouting about peace," remarked Father Tim. "Those that are doing the shouting have got all they want now. Of course, they want peace. This is what I say. Let them give back what doesn't belong to them, then we'll have peace. Let them make salt, or whatever it is they want to do in India."

Mention of prohibition set off a cache of rhetorical dynamite. His big right hand came down with a thud on the arm of his easy chair. "All this talk about prohibition! Men didn't drink things before that they do now, and I didn't have to lock the church doors for eight months just to keep the drunks from wandering into the first warm place they found. The prohibitionists are hypocrites and so are the antiprohibitionists. They say they don't want the corner saloon. All right, put it in the middle of the block. In the old days a man could walk into a saloon and shake hands with anyone he found there. Now he's apt to get punched in the face."

One of the reporters, noticing the radio along the wall, sounded him out on the subject of radio. Father Tim told them that he didn't have much time to listen to the radio but he liked to hear football games, especially Notre Dame games, and to listen to symphonies and operas. "The trouble with radio is there's not enough singing of Irish songs. Sure, they seem to think there are only two of them, 'Come Back to Erin', and 'Believe Me, If All Those Endearing Young Charms.'"

His thoughts flew back to the depression. "There are too many men in St. Louis who look like Cassius." The blank look on the faces of his listeners told him that Cassius didn't register; so he took the occasion to give them a little exhortation.

"You talk about culture, and yet none of you read Shakespeare and the Bible. I doubt if you know the difference between Moses and Aaron. But as to the quotation which I mention, 'Yon Cassius has a lean and hungry look,' it is just as true today as it was when Shakespeare made Julius Caesar say that 'such men are dangerous.'"

Then he let a secret out of the bag. "I intend to open a Free

Lunch Station in the basement of the school next month. Now, I don't want people to get the idea that I am establishing a bread line. I just want to do all I can to help those who are hungry and would like a place to stop in for a while to get warm and have a cup of good hot coffee. I intend to keep the Station open as long as people keep coming."

Father Dempsey was as good as his word. On Monday, November 16, 1931, the Free Lunch Station began a service which was to make it internationally famous. He himself was behind the serving table to make his more than thousand guests feel at home. His friendly smile probably meant more to them than the coffee and bread served. Eight and one were the hours for serving. Women in the neighborhood gladly volunteered to help at the Station.

As the weeks rolled around, the number of guests increased. Providentially so did the donations of foodstuffs and money. Fifteen women and girls and seven men were kept busy as potato peelers, dishwashers, cooks, and dispensers.

The first Thanksgiving Day was memorable. A wet snow made things uncomfortable for the men in the line, especially for those whose soles were worn out or thin. The men forgot their discomfort for the moment when they saw Father Tim standing in the snow, waiting to shake each man's hand and to wish each of them a happy Thanksgiving Day. He told a reporter, "I am elated. I never was more happy. The Food Station is really meeting a need. There is no doubt now that it will go on. I never did have any doubt." When asked about his organization, he said with a bit of fire, "'Organization' is a word I don't like. We have order, which is much better."

Standing in the snow proved harmful to a constitution already weakened from the strain of managing the various institutions, taking care of parolees, settling strikes and gang wars, and opening the new Food Station. He found himself in St. John's Hospital with high blood pressure and distraught nerves at the time of the Silver Jubilee of the Men's Hotel in December.

"I expect to be out shortly, but I think that I will be as thin as a glass of water," he told his friends. Back at work again he noticed the growing number of colored folks in the line. He used to comment on the perfection of a Negro's ear. It was a matter of great wonder to him. He noted too that the depression was hitting the colored folks harder than it hit the whites. That's what made him think of opening a home for the colored.

The miracle of the lunchroom stimulated some keen editorial comments in the *Globe-Democrat* on March 22, 1932:

> Students of sociology have shaken their heads this winter as they read of the thousands gathered day after day at Father Tim Dempsey's emergency lunchroom. Where so many are receiving help, there is danger that somebody will get a free meal who already has been fed. Some strict constructionists of lenten rules doubtless feel the same way on learning that meat is going to be served to these homeless and poorly clad men in Holy Week.
>
> After all, it appeals to the average man that in these days, with everything reduced to scientific and business rules, there is one place where humanity takes precedence of sociological data. It may be demoralizing to some individuals, but it is a pleasant return to old standards. The biblical commands on feeding the hungry are not completely out of date. And since there is nothing in them to show whether those fed should be white or of some other race, Father Dempsey has opened a shelter for negroes in addition to feeding the whites.
>
> Some men hanker to be president. Others work themselves to death trying to become millionaires. There must be many who, if they had the choice, would rather be Father Tim Dempsey with a heart full of love for his fellow men and knowledge that thousands of his fellow men have hearts full of love for him.

The editorial plainly tells its own story. Father Tim's card-catalogue, as we have said before, was his own tenacious memory. He did not pester the reticent in an effort to load it with what to him, in his method of work, was a mass of inconsequential details. If a person in trouble wished to talk, he would find a sympathetic listener in Father Tim. Critical of modern methods but not rejecting the good in them, he was a man of direct action like Christ. He used to say: "Imagine our Lord at the feeding of the 5000 saying to some poor woman, 'You knew you were going to be gone all day. Why didn't you have sense enough to bring something to eat with you?'; or looking at some ill-clad old man and remarking, 'That bloke doesn't deserve anything to eat.'" To the often rather crude social-work element of that early day he good humoredly referred, in his pleasant Irish brogue, by saying: "They're full of bosh!"

That's why one fair-minded and judicious critic of Father Dempsey's social work, himself a believer in the necessity of scientific methods, summarized his estimate in the brief sentence, "Father Dempsey was ahead of his time when he started out and behind his time toward the end of his life; he was to social service what the horse-and-buggy doctor was to medicine." This same critic, a Jew, spent many hours with Father Dempsey. On one occasion he stimulated a religious discussion that lasted from nine o'clock at night till three or four the next morning by quoting Nietzsche's definition: "A Christian is a person who worships a dead Jew and hates a live one." When he named a number of bad clergymen in history, Father Tim, attempting no whitewash, simply and emphatically said of each of them, "That man should have been hanged!"

This same blunt honesty and frankness knocked the wind out a certain non-Catholic woman who was being introduced to Father Tim one time. At the time of introduction she tossed her head in a superior manner and with no effort at sweetening her tones told him straight to his face, "I don't like priests." Father Tim smiled and looked her in the eye, "Well, Mrs., if you knew them as well as I do, you'd like them a lot less." Eventually she became a Catholic.

The Lunchroom continued its salutary relief work. The newspapers generously publicized the needs and results of the Station. Father Dempsey felt that he owed a debt of gratitude to the *Star-Times*, *Post-Dispatch*, and the *Globe-Democrat* and also to the Catholic papers, but especially to the *Globe*.

So when this paper moved to new quarters on Twelfth Street, he sent a letter of congratulations.

> As one of your older readers whose daily perusal of your valued paper extends considerably back into the last century, I desire to add my hearty congratulations to the thousands of good wishes which you are receiving on your removal to the spacious building on Twelfth Street, a landmark in all St. Louis.
>
> There is more than felicitation in my expression, as I share in your joy which comes as the crown of good works. The old building was christened "The Temple of Truth" by that great editor, the late Joseph B. McCullagh. May his worthy successors continue to carry on the same principles, as you have been doing, managing in a "temple" of greater opportunity to do even greater good.
>
> Personally the charities which a kindly Providence has permitted myself to promote could perhaps never have reached their present proportions, in helping those whom I know to be in need, had it not been for the *Globe-Democrat's* willingness to cooperate in all our undertakings for God's poor "from the cradle to the grave." In the name of the poor, I thank you, and in the name of truth and free speech, I congratulate you. My congratulations and good wishes likewise to E. Lansing Ray, to Casper Yost, and to Joe McAuliffe.

Not everybody was as friendly toward the Free Lunchroom as were the newspapers. Some opposed it on the grounds that the method of individual home feeding was cheaper. Father Tim's answer to this was to show by statistics that the cost per meal at the Lunchroom was less than two cents. Others argued that the mass plan of feeding invited hoboes and riffraff from the surrounding country. Father Tim was not particularly disturbed by the arrival of hungry men from other parts as long as they behaved themselves around St. Patrick's. Respect for "the big fellow with the black-thorn stick" acted as a restraint on dangerously ebullient spirits. In January, 1932, he boasted, "There never yet has been a fight in the line since the day we started. Only three times have we had to have men taken out of the line because of their having too much Volstead in them."

Some people objected on the score of money, arguing that, if Father Dempsey got all the food he needed for nothing, he should not need money. Father Tim's first answer to this was that he had to buy some of the food. Secondly, he said that money was spent in salaries, for gas, electric light, water, tobacco, soap powder, laundry, paint, lumber, plumbing, welding, utensils, and the like. Thirdly, he told how often he was importuned for financial help. In two or three hours he might receive twenty requests. The majority of people were satisfied with his answers to the objections against the Lunchroom, and proved their satisfaction by rallying generously to the support of all his works.

During Lent a number of women made sandwiches for the men in the line. An Italian woman, the mother of seventeen children, was the chief cook. One day on a visit to the Lunchroom Father Tim aired a bit of erudition about the Middle Ages as he watched the women make the sandwiches. "You are going back to the knightly definition of a lady. You are becoming 'loaf-givers,' which was what 'lady' meant in the time of the Crusaders. I am not a modernist. I refuse to call you 'women.' I shall call you 'ladies.' "

In May he was worried about the continuation of the Lunchroom. On May 22 four-hundred men were turned away hungry. Father Tim's heart was sad as he stood on the front steps of the parish house and told the men that the food supply had run out. "I hope you're not very hungry, boys, and I hope this will be the only time it can be said that an Irish priest had to refuse food to anyone." One of the ragged men shouted, "That's all right, Father. Thanks for all the meals we've had."

The publicizing of this incident led to increased benefactions. Commenting on this one day, Father Tim added a bit of erudition. "You know, in North China up there where the desert has taken the place of one-time abundant forests, which have all been cut down by man, there is a greeting, a quite common greeting, they say. It is this: instead of saying, 'God bless you,' or 'God save all here,' the natives of China meet one another and say, 'Good morning, have you breakfasted?'

And if they have, they reply, 'Ah, yes, I am among the fortunate.' So it is this week with my men here."

When a reporter asked him how he was able to operate at such a low cost as one-half to two cents per meal, Father Tim explained: "The first reason . . . is that there are no professional trained workers paid. The services of the Sisters of Charity cost nothing. They distribute milk, vegetables, and other necessities to an average of seventy families daily, white and colored, this distribution taking place after the noon meal. The second reason is that we do not attempt to solve any individual 'case' problems, and we have no waiting 'intake' department for applicants, nor do we make analysis of methods used in caring for hungry men." The reporter couldn't help noticing the good-natured venom in Father Tim's tone. "The third reason is that we have no participation in any fund, either from the Free Bridge, or from policemen's salaries, or from barber chairs."

Although managing the Lunchroom did not cost so much in terms of money, it was costing plenty in terms of Father Tim's health. He needed a change. While he was recuperating in Ireland during September and October, he sat down one day on the veranda of the hotel at Birr, Offaly, and wrote a letter to the men in the line. The assistant pastor read it to the men: "I am feeling about twenty-one years of age. The fresh air and blue skies of Ireland are doing me more good than all the doctors, just as they told me it would when I started." When the assistant had finished, one of the men shouted, "Hurray for Father Tim!" and in a few seconds the whole line was cheering, "Hurray for Father Tim!"

He returned to St. Louis in the latter part of October, much restored in health and voluble about Ireland. When asked about his relief plans, he said, "Son, I never had a plan in my life. All I'm going to do is to keep right on feeding those who come day by day, by the grace of God. You know, somehow everybody is good to me. Sure, there never was a man crossed the ocean who had as many people good to him as they are to me."

With a good deal of satisfaction he published the first annual report on the Lunchroom. A total of 1,228,674 free meals had been served. His satisfaction was enhanced by the fact that he had kept the friendship of owners of low-priced restaurants in the neighborhood. "But aren't you taking away their trade?" someone asked. "Not at all, not at all; they help support me. Two of them have given their places Irish names. They are all my friends. I believe if anyone should say a word against me to one of them, that man would never sin again."

The number of men in the line continued to grow. Every nationality seemed to be represented. Even a turbaned Hindu, stolid, brown-skinned, and hungry, put in an appearance one day. When Father Tim saw the Hindu, he remarked, "This is an international line. That man has been unable to practice the Hindu art of suspended animation, but becomes hungry just as if he were an Occidental."

It was pretty much a dumb and unseeing queue that stretched north on Sixth Street, west on O'Fallon to the alley between Sixth and Seventh, south on the alley to Biddle, and east on Biddle to Sixth. Men who have been walking around starving are usually not brilliant conversationalists.

There were some wrecks of humanity whose alcohol-bloated faces and filthy speech betrayed lives badly lived. There were men with honest faces, deep-lined from living up to serious responsibilities, whose threadbare clothes were of a quality that spoke of days of affluence before the depression. Father Tim could single out lawyers, doctors, businessmen, and day laborers whose stooped shoulders and worried faces told the story of the depression without words. Many men in search of work would stop at the "soup kitchen" in order to save a few dimes for their families. In the words of O. A. Danielson in "The Man Without a Hoe":

> Bowed by hunger gnawing at his vitals
> And without the hoe to lean upon,
> He pursues his weary, useless quest for work,
> The emptiness of famine in his face. . . .

Is this poor man, hollow-eyed and gaunt,
The end and purpose of our generous plan?
Of years devoted to the gain of knowledge?
Was it for this he toiled arduously to learn?
Without hoe or tools, what profit to have learned
To cultivate the soil for the rich harvest?

Yesterday — a valued honest citizen
Of his native land; working faithfully
To develop its boundless resources.
Today — unwanted, pitiful, vagrant,
Forsaken by those who were by him enriched.

In that line were men who had to wrap gunny sacks around their worn-out shoes to keep their feet from freezing. Tragedy lived and breathed on Sixth Street, the Sixth Street of Father Tim. Men asked themselves why these things should be in an economy geared to produce all that man could use, even more than man could use. Men shook their heads savagely at a system of distribution which didn't distribute. Perhaps there was something wrong with liberal economics; perhaps the Popes were right. Were men made for machines, or were machines made for men?

Educated men asked themselves whether perhaps Ruskin was not right when he said that "Men may be beaten, chained, tormented, yoked like cattle, slaughtered like summer flies, and yet remain in one sense, and the best sense, free. But to smother their souls within them, to blight and hew into rotting pollards the suckling branches of their human intelligence, to make the flesh and skin which, after the worm's work on it, is to see God, into leathern thongs to yoke machinery with — this it is to be slave-masters indeed. . . . To feel their souls withering within them, unthanked, to find their whole being sunk into an unrecognized abyss, to be counted off into a heap of mechanism, numbered with its wheels, and weighed with its hammer strokes — this nature bade not — this God blesses not — this humanity for no long time is able to endure."

Occasionally a bit of comic relief was injected into the tragedy of Sixth Street. One day two men who evidently had great mutual confidence cut each other's hair on the march. One trimmed the neck and ears of the man in front of him, and then they switched positions. Service while you walk.

Although Father Tim did not believe in stuffing religion down a man's throat, he was anxious to do something of a spiritual nature for the men in the free lunch line. So when the Rev. John P. Markoe, S.J., suggested the plan of a continuous mission with a daily instruction for twenty minutes at noon and Benediction of the Most Blessed Sacrament, he welcomed the idea warmly. The scheme was a practical answer to Pope Pius XI's plea in *Mens Nostra* to bring the spiritual exercises to the poor.

After advertising the mission by handbills and pulpit announcements, Father Tim opened the mission with an introductory talk on September 11, 1933, using as themes the scriptural passages, "The poor have the gospel preached to them," and "Go out into the highways and invite those who have not on the wedding garment," and commenting that he himself had gone into the highways with the result that the "highwaymen" were his friends. "I intend to hold them for the Lord," he said. "Not by bread alone does man live, but by every word that proceeds from the mouth of God. I desire all to hear the word of God. There will be no distinction of race, creed, or color, but everyone is invited to attend these services without compulsion. The baneful influence of those organizations which would have men seek happiness while ignoring religion is to be opposed."

When Father Markoe was forced to give up the work in February, 1934, the Rev. Francis J. Rudden, S.J., his coworker from the start, continued the mission for some months. Many baptisms and confessions were the fruit of their labors. Later, Sunday afternoon instructions, given by laymen and by Jesuit seminarians, were offered as a help to the men in the line. During Lent each year the Rev. Theodore Hegemann, S.J., assistant pastor at near-by St. Joseph's church, conducted daily devotions.

On Mother's Day, May 13, 1934, Father Tim's guests in the line were reminded of the meaning of the day. He encouraged those whose mothers were still alive to write on this day, and even offered them writing paper and pencils. Some of the men put their heads together for a bit of sidewalk harmony on "Mother Machree" and "Mother o' Mine." Nearly every man wore with a certain self-consciousness a little paper flower on his breast.

One day an unemployed man from Pittsburgh was talking to Father Dempsey. His old clothes were dirty from a train trip on the boxcars; his thin face had a hungry look; a thick stand of whiskers was waiting to be harvested.

"And how are things in Pittsburgh, my good man?"

"Worse than here, Father. There's no work for them that want it, and they're laying off men everywhere."

"Is it so bad as that?"

"Yes, Father. In fact, things are so bad that the Bishop himself laid off forty priests last week."

The laying off of men continued for some time in various parts of the country. Times were slow to get better. The need for a Free Lunch Room remained. During the blackest depths of the depression as many as 13,000 free meals were served in a single day. In one week during August, 1933, the total of free meals was 82,455. By the time of Father Tim's death the astronomical figure of 5,673,917 was reached. The meals were not always of a sort that would tempt an epicure; in fact, at times when Father Tim was not able to keep close tab on the activities of his helpers and donors, the food was far from savory.

Father Dempsey never intended this bit of charitable relief as a substitute for distributive and social justice. He wasn't running the Free Lunch Room to provide the "haves" with an opportunity to salve their consciences for their unjust conduct toward the "have-nots." His whole life had been a struggle to win justice for the poor and the downtrodden; but he did believe that justice had to be sweetened by charity.

He realized with Father Raoul Plus, S.J., "that human justice without charity is often only a barbarous virtue, that a sufficient wage given by a cold heart is more humiliating than the alms of only a half-penny inspired by real affection. . . . If right alone ruled the universe, we should have a citadel of cut-throats. What is the true meaning of the Roman legal phrase: *Summum jus, summa injuria?* Strict justice, supreme injustice, which implies that if justice only be considered, there is a risk of it running astray in practice. A virtue that has to be portrayed with a sword at its side is hardly reassuring unless a sister virtue watches beside it and keeps that sword in its sheath – the name of this sister virtue is charity."

Father Tim saw hungry men, thirsty men, cold men. Himself a man of direct action, with a deeply sympathetic heart, he fed these hungry men, gave drink to these thirsty men, clothed these almost naked men, and housed them in a warm building. He would leave it to the "experts" to solve the basic problems of a dislocated economy; he had enough to do. The depression, bringing with it more intense suffering for the colored folks, had given him yet another job, the care of another institution.

Chapter 13

"TELL ME, WHERE'S MY PLACE?"

COLORED people in the United States have long been asking the question that the Rev. Daniel A. Lord, S.J., put to music and introduced to the world in his Social Order Follies through the medium of Arthur Burgette's appealing baritone voice:

> But say, white man,
>   Tell me to my face,
> Ah say, white man,
>   Tell me, where's my place?
>
> For I'm a man who lives and loves,
>   Who clings to home and wife,
>
> Who sings to sleep
>   The baby on his knee;
> Who tells his child
>   His country made him free.
>
> You struck the chains and bade me lift my face,
>   But tell me, white man,
> Tell me, are the *depths* my place?

Colored men who had fought on the battlefields of France in 1918 in order "to make the world safe for democracy" returned bearing in their hearts the determination that the democracy they fought for should be concretely applied to their race in the United States. No, the depths were not their place.

Perhaps social investigators could point to low scores in mental tests, to the wretched condition of their southern shacks, to their unhealthy and crowded conditions in city slums, to their low state of health in general, to their high death rate, and to a disproportionately high percentage of delinquency and crime. The educated colored man and his white defender had an answer, a poetic answer: these were the fruits that grew on the trees of discrimination and lack of opportunity. Give the colored man and woman a chance, said they. Isn't the colored man truly a man? they asked. Isn't he an American, honoring the same red, white, and blue, devoted to those principles and ideals embodied in the Constitution in regard to freedom of religion, of speech, of the press, and of assembly? Isn't he quite commonly a Christian, a man who can look at the motto on a silver dollar, "In God We Trust," without his conscience reproaching him? Why, then, this un-American exclusion from voting in certain areas? from equal educational opportunities? from public institutions? Why, then, this un-American segregation as to residence, public conveyances, and places of amusement? Why deny him equal working rights? Interested partisans argued back and forth, but the condition of the colored people was not notably improved during the 1920's and the 1930's. Experts continued to talk about the "Negro problem."

For Father Tim Dempsey there was no Negro problem, there was a Negro opportunity. In Ireland there had been neither a Negro problem nor a Negro opportunity; one didn't find any colored folks in Ireland. But from the time his boat docked in New York harbor in 1891 till his dying day, he was to meet plenty of colored folk. When it came to dealing with people, he was color-blind. It didn't matter to him that the color of people is ascribable to a subcutaneous tissue, the pigmentum, which is black in Negroes and red in whites, while the skin itself is parchment gray in both cases. He didn't bother his head to speculate as to why colored people were colored. But his faith caused him to speculate about their temporal and eternal welfare.

Looking at them from the viewpoint of Christ, he saw

in their color no obstacle to membership in Christ's Mystical Body. He knew, too, that Christ did not say, "Whatever you do to one of these My least *white* brethren, that you do to Me." He knew that "when the roll is called up yonder" a man wouldn't be asked, "Are you white?," but "Are you God's friend?" To Father Tim as to St. Paul: "There is neither Jew nor Greek; there is neither bond nor free; there is neither male nor female. For you are all one in Christ Jesus." And Father Tim would add explicitly: "There is neither black nor white." But he was no mere theological or philosophical speculator; his was that practical Christianity which is talked about so much by people who are neither practical nor Christian.

Opportunities to prove the practical nature of his Christianity in regard to the Negroes came early in his pastorate at St. Patrick's. The colored trek to the cities in the last part of the nineteenth century and the first three decades of the twentieth was part of a general movement away from the land common to all industrial countries. A few trickled into St. Patrick's around 1900; thousands settled in the lower St. Louis area between 1916 and 1919 and between 1921 and 1924. Discontented with southern conditions, they were looking for new opportunities and freedom from social discrimination.

Those who settled in the shadow of old St. Patrick's church quickly found out that they had a friend in Father Tim. The majority of them were not Catholic and were inclined to be suspicious of "dat Catlik priest." But his openhearted manner broke down their reserve. They found out that he was as willing to help them as he was to help the whites. He would try to get work for them; he would see to it that they had hospital attention; he wouldn't refuse them food or drink. They were as welcome in church as their white "brethren." When a sufficient number became Catholics, he designated one of the Sunday Masses as their own. He encouraged the formation of religious societies and clubs.

As Spanish ladies in Carthagena in the seventeenth century complained that the smell of the Negroes who had attended St. Peter Claver's daybreak Mass clung tenaciously to the church and, in the words of Arnold Lunn, rendered its interior insupportable to sensitive nostrils for the remainder of the day, so some of the white members of St. Patrick's parish complained to Father Tim. Such an objection made about as much of an impression on him as shotgun pellets would on the side of a modern battleship. Not that he was insensible to the delicate refinements of life, no; but a proper sense of values had to be maintained. He may have been tempted to remind the complainers that the colored folk found the smell of whites equally obnoxious but refused to complain about it.

For some years he had in his service as laundress an immense colored woman whose teeth were as white as the clothes she turned out and whose thick lips always seemed to be playing with an imminent smile. No one would hang a medal on Matti's expansive breast for intellectual brilliancy, but she did a good job on the clothes. Father Tim liked her. One day a group of Father Tim's guests were boasting about their academic degrees and their superior education. He didn't like to hear anyone brag about his education, so he decided to puncture their academic balloon.

"Matti," he called, "come here."

Matti waddled in and bowed her most gracious southern bow. Father Tim introduced her to his guests with a triumphant smile: "This is Matti. I believe Matti was a graduate of Georgia Tech!" This sudden conferring of a degree for technical skill at ironing surprised the humble Matti and humbled the surprised guests.

At the time of the establishment of the Men's Hotel, 1906, there was no need for a similar home for colored men. But the depression years, 1929 and following, created a very real need. Father Tim had talked to colored men in the bread line and learned how hard up they were for a place to sleep. When employers found it necessary to lay off men, the colored men found themselves walking the streets first. If they had been of a disposition to worry unreasonably, they might have ended up dangling from ropes or with their lifeblood pouring out of slashed wrists; but the majority had enough faith and patience to support life even when it seemed unsupportable. They had the spirit of Uncle Tom's philosophy of life, expressed in his poem, "Jes' Keep de Lawd in Mind":

Thar's a way o' keepin' good, As de Massah says we should—
'Tain't so hard, I think, as folks is always sayin'.
Don' consis' in foolish fears, Don' consis' in sheddin' tears,
Nor in wearin' out yo' knees in jes' a-prayin'.
It's an easy way, I fin'—*Jes' you keep de Lawd in min'.*
Be you workin' hard at somethin', or jes' playin'.
Fo' de Lawd—He's pow'ful wise—Nothin' hidden from His eyes,
An' His lovin' Heart sure knows our ev'ry cravin'.
'Cause He made us—you and me—So He knows us—cain't you see?
Yes, it grieves Him fo' to see us misbehavin' . . .
But we're work o' His own Hands, An' our ways He understan's,
'Cause it 'pears He holds us all wu'th de savin'.
With de Lawd a-watchin' o'er, what if trouble's at mah door?
Ev'ry cloud is sure to show its silver linin'.
So I keeps de Lawd in min'—It's an easy way, I fin'—
'Tain't no other joy but Him fo' which I'm pinin'.
Seems Ah want Him mo' and more as Ah nears de heaven-shore
Whar His lovelight leadin' me is always shinin'.

Such a comforting philosophy, however, was not sufficient in itself to keep a poor colored man from freezing at night or from feeling the pains of hunger. The normal man can't live on mere lovelight as he "nears de heaven-shore." In the winter he needs warm clothing and warm blankets and a warm place to sleep; he needs food and drink the year around; he may need medicine, tobacco, a doctor's attention. With all his ideals Father Tim was enough of a realist to face these commonplace facts. He began to angle for a building to house the needy colored man.

In February, 1932, the Arndt Manufacturing Company

offered the use of a two-story brick building, rent free, at 1127 North Sixth Street, about two doors south of the church. He took the offer. At the age of 65, weakened in health by the long strain of a full, laborious life, and already burdened with the management of a fistful of institutional works, the mellowed Monsignor was busy with a new venture, St. Patrick's Home for the Colored.

When reporters asked him about the home, he explained: "The Negroes get as cold as anybody else these nights. White men are cared for in the Workingmen's Hotel, but it will be a Godsend to let the colored man who is needy have a place to sleep in comfort. It will not be a Lake Shore Hotel, and I haven't got space for a sun parlor, but there'll be a fine breeze from the river if anyone wants a breeze."

The religious and secular press cooperated in advertising the immediate needs of the new institution. Stoves, fuel, mattresses, beds, blankets, and other necessaries donated by people whose love for others was more than skin-deep began to be unloaded at the Sixth Street address. A Mr. William Brown was engaged as clerk. By February 20 the place was ready for operation. Father Tim said, "I think I'll call my guests Knights of St. Patrick in memory of that splendid order which made St. Patrick's Day memorable with a great parade." Apparently he never reconciled himself to the abandonment of the glamorous parade on St. Patrick's Day.

By February 25 the newspapers were able to say, "There were 169 in the house last night." The papers forgot to mention that some of these 169 got their night's rest on the floor. Even the floor sleepers probably felt that this was better than a night on the highway or in a railroad tunnel or in a breezy warehouse. Satisfaction with the home is proved by the fact that between February 20, 1932, and January 1, 1933, a total of 69,950 free lodgings were provided.

But October, 1933, brought a rude jolt to Father Tim and to his colored friends. His harboring of the colored harborless would have to cease, at least in the present building. The company needed the space again with the revival of their business. Father Tim commented with mixed feelings, "I am glad to see business reviving, but the colored men, as they were the first to feel the pinch of the depression, are likely to be the last to gain full employment, so we must find a new home for them."

But his appeals for the use of some vacant building or other in the vicinity of St. Patrick's church were of no avail. The colored men had to shift for themselves. The intention of establishing another home for them went to the grave with Father Tim. Only a day or so before his death he had asked his clerk, Mr. Bernard Gantney, to step off the empty lot directly across the street from the church with a view to determining whether there would be sufficient space for the construction of a home for the colored.

Some of the Negroes had strange ideas about the wealth of the Church and of Father Dempsey. A steady customer, call him Mose, was talking to a pal of his, call him Rastus, who had just arrived via boxcar from Chicago. Rastus was hungry and tired. "Mose," he asked, holding his stomach and rolling his eyes, "wheah in de Lawd's name kin Ah git somethin' to eat?"

"We all kin go up to Faddah Dempsey's."

"Who's dat?"

"He's a Catlik Faddah who all feeds us poor devils who ain't got no work."

Rastus, a bit excited at hearing the word "Catlik," asked, "Do yuh all have to join up?"

"Naw, you doan have to join up. Faddah Dempsey doan want yuh, anyhow. Yuh ain't got no money."

There is no doubt that Father Tim was interested in money. Desire of this is the root of all evils; it also can be the means to many good things. His heart was not attached to it; he spent it almost as fast as he got it on those poor people who needed immediate help and on his institutional works. Now one of these institutions was no more, his home for the colored; but he still was on the side of interracial justice and charity.

Chapter 14

THE LAW AND ANGELS OF MERCY

TO FATHER DEMPSEY law, divine or human, and the symbols of law were to be respected. He recognized all authority as coming from God. The wholesale flouting of law and authority was as much of a puzzle to him as the use of scientific terminology in the discussion of social welfare. He used to shake his big head in bewilderment at the folly of men and women who looked for happiness in a way of living as disordered as a child's playroom the week after Christmas. But he never despaired of those who walked the low road. "Glory be to God," said he, "there's good in every man, and with the help of God we'll find it."

While Father Tim was searching for the good in every man, human society was knocking off the bad rough edges of those who chose to violate reasonable laws. The criminal who laughed at abstract laws might quake before a policeman. Law in the concrete meant policemen on the sidewalks. Authority in the concrete meant a billy club and a revolver.

Father Dempsey's work threw him into intimate contact with the guardians of law and order. His own brother, Tom, who later became a priest and was pastor at St. Patrick, Mo., was a mounted policeman for years. His brother, Frank, was a detective. His one-armed brother, Vincent, was a lawyer. The long and only partially successful struggle to pacify rival gangs in the 1920's brought him into close association with the police. Because of his exceptional memory for names and faces, police inspectors in the United

States and other countries often called on him to identify photographs of suspected criminals. He was a frequent caller at the city jail, police headquarters, and the Carr Street station, and was on intimate terms with successive police chiefs and with successive bosses on Carr Street, among whom were Captains O'Malley, Nally, and Callahan.

Bursting in on Captain O'Malley one day, Father Dempsey waved an anonymous blackmail letter before the astonished eyes of the captain. The blackmailer commanded Father Tim to appear at Eads bridge with a big sum of money at a certain hour of the night. "Aye," affirmed Father Tim with a vehement shaking of his head and an ominous gesture with his blackthorn stick, "it's there I'll be, and that man will be sorry."

O'Malley objected. The pastor's life was too valuable to take any such chances. Better to have a certain patrolman disguise himself as the pastor and show up at the time specified.

Father Tim stared at Captain O'Malley in surprise. Then with a good deal of emphasis, "I'll never disgrace the cloth by putting it on a police officer. I'll be there myself."

It took a bit of O'Malley oratory to persuade him not to appear on Eads bridge. A patrolman wearing civilian clothes was sent. But nothing happened; the whole thing was a hoax. Father Tim was glad he didn't go. There's no thrill in standing on Eads bridge alone in the wee hours with the cold fingers of the north wind tearing at one's clothes.

On another occasion he was called to a notorious dive on an errand of a spiritual nature. He took a layman along as companion. While Father Tim was ministering to the dying person inside the place, the layman patiently waited outside. A policeman happened along. "Git along," he commanded the man. Offering no protest, Father Tim's companion moved around the corner. As soon as the officer had passed, he came back to his post. The officer happened along again. "All right, you, git movin'!" The man held his ground. "I'm waiting for Father Dempsey." Understanding in the remark an insult to his priestly friend, the policeman promptly beat the man up. There must have been some profuse apologies when the misunderstanding was finally corrected.

At times Father Dempsey exasperated police and detectives by his seeming unconcern about apprehending suspects. They should have realized that wasn't his job. One time he jarred his own brother, Sergeant Frank. An intermittent lodger at the Men's Hotel was suspected of stealing an overcoat. Frank sought his brother's help in apprehending the man. Quite noncommittal about the suspect's location, Father Tim asked whose overcoat had been stolen.

"The Archbishop's—taken right off the hook in the sacristy of the cathedral."

Father Tim chuckled, his eyes sparkled. "Who could better afford to lose an overcoat?" Sergeant Frank walked away in despair. What could one do with a man like that?

In general, Father Tim was cooperative in so far as cooperation was consistent with his priestly calling. In 1935 he cooperated by allowing his Pipers' Band to appear on the program of the police circus at the Coliseum. He was as proud of this band as he was of his Workingmen's Union at the Men's Hotel. They made a big hit with the thousands of people at the police circus. A short while after their performance Captain Andrew Aylward helped the cause of higher music along by sending Father Tim a check for three hundred dollars as a token of appreciation for their work at the circus.

When friends would kid Father Tim about the non-Irish names in his Irish Pipers' Band, and his Fife, Drum, and Bugle Corps, he would say, "Ah yes, b'y, but remember, b'y, the mother of every son of them is Irish." A big bus, donated for the use of the Pipers, with its Killarney green base, its silver top, and its warning painted on the silver along the curve of the roof, "Faugh A Ballagh," Gaelic for "Clear the way," the battle-cry of the Connaught Rangers, was a familiar sight on the streets of St. Louis. Father Tim was proud of his Fife, Drum, and Bugle Corps with its personnel of one bass drummer, eight snare drummers, twenty fifers, three buglers, a leader, flagbearers, and six pipers.

The police would do just about anything they could for Father Tim. On one occasion Radio Station WEW of St. Louis University had signed up a very capable musician. Shortly before he was to make his radio appearance, he was jailed for having stolen the instrument he intended to use. The manager of WEW wrung his hands and pulled his hair in desperation until one of the Jesuit Fathers suggested that he call Father Tim who was at the time ill in St. John's Hospital. Father Tim answered the call with a brief, "I'll fix that up." The pilfering musician appeared on the program.

Sometimes Father Dempsey's guests took such liberties with his name that they found themselves in trouble with the police. One of the men at the hotel used Father Tim's name in forging a check for $100. Father Tim had good reasons for fastening the guilt on a certain Irishman. When a policeman called at the rectory and asked for the name of the man, Father Tim, after stalling him off for a while, finally said, "His name is Paddy O'Shaughnessy, and he's from my own county in Ireland."

"Thank you, Father. What if he had come from somewhere else?"

"Well, instead of being easy on him, I'd say, hang him!"

Since he lived in a rather tough neighborhood, Father Dempsey often had to be his own policeman. More than once he grabbed his blackthorn stick and hastened to a saloon to straighten out some leering wife-beater whose strong arm tactics had sent the bruised and crying woman to the rectory. Sometimes he had to teach tough rooming-house operators a lesson. One day he was startled by a sudden scuffle in front of him. Out of the door of a rooming house rolled a sick-looking man on the receiving end of a swift kick. He landed in the gutter. The rooming-house operator glared in anger at the prone figure and drew back his leg to kick his victim again. Father Tim's strong grip closed on his arm.

"Who are you?" the kicking expert demanded angrily.

"Timothy Dempsey," said Father Tim bluntly, "and for fear you'll forget, here's a reminder." His big right fist sent the operator sprawling. The language of fists was the only language that some of the people in the neighborhood understood. So even Father Tim used their muscular vernacular at times.

That the mutual relations of the police and the St. Patrick's pastor were in general cordial is clear from a "thank you" letter that Father Tim sent to the chief of police in 1934 after he had received a gift of $6,021.85 from the policemen.

My dear Chief:

I wish I could thank every member of the Police Department personally for the magnificent evidence of interest in my work. I can only say your princely offering (the largest I ever received) will never be forgotten.

I now feel pleased with myself when I recall my more than 40 years' friendly relations with every officer whom it was my privilege to meet. No matter who he was or whence he came, I always had a friendly feeling for every man in the department — from Chief Harrigan of long ago, to the last probationary.

These thoughts, I pray, will always be in the mind of

Yours sincerely and gratefully,
(Signed) Timothy Dempsey

His friendly relations with the police were equaled or even surpassed by his relations with the hospital Sisters, "God's noblest daughters." From his earliest days at St. Patrick's they had taken care of the sick he sent to them, often free of charge. Frequent personal breakdowns of health, especially in later years, forced him to avail himself of their kindly ministrations. He spent a short time at Mullanphy Hospital in 1911 to rest after his overexertion in the founding of the Day Nursery and the Women's Hotel. The winter of 1931–1932 brought him a long siege in St. John's Hospital, a siege brightened by the countless kind acts of Sisters and nurses and especially by a surprise program presented in his honor on the Feast of St. Timothy, January 24.

Tears came to his eyes as he heard himself called "Our Soggarth Aroon," that is, priest of my heart, in a poem written by one of the Sisters.

Friend of the friendless poor,
Soggarth Aroon,
Grim want is at our door,
Soggarth Aroon,
Minister of Christ Who said,
"When the children ask for bread,
Who would give a stone instead?"
Soggarth Aroon,

The poem goes on to praise his work for the poor and concludes with the words:

When depression's gone for aye,
Soggarth Aroon,
And there dawns the eternal day,
Soggarth Aroon,
In that land by strife unmarred
May your Captain, Christ our Lord,
Be your bountiful reward,
Soggarth Aroon,

During this same siege one of the doctors told him that a blood test would have to be made. Opposed to tests and charts and such paraphernalia in general, Father Tim with characteristic vivacity shot back, "Why test my blood? There's nothing but good blood where I come from."

He was somewhat afraid of the venerable Jesuit chaplain at St. John's, the late Father John Mathery. He would say to a visiting Father, "That man Mathery is a saint. Glory be to God, the old man could smell a mortal sin on the fourth floor all the way from the first! You hear my confession, Father. I don't want to shock the old man."

He treasured Captain Jack Crawford's tribute to Sisters and had it published in his Hotel Magazine.

On all God's green and beautiful earth there are no purer, no nobler, no more kind-hearted and self-sacrificing women than those who wear the somber garb of the Catholic sisters. During the Civil War I had many opportunities for observing their noble and heroic work, not only in camp and hospital, but in the death-swept field of battle.

Right in the fiery front of dreadful war, where bullets hissed in maddening glee, and shot and shell flew madly by with demoniac shrieks, where dead and mangled forms lay with pale, blood-flecked faces, yet wearing the scowl of battle, I have seen the black-robed sisters moving over the field, their solicitous faces wet with tears of sympathy, administering to the wants of the wounded and whispering words of comfort into the ears soon to be deafened by the cold, implacable hand of death.

How many a veteran of the war who wore the blue or the gray can yet recall the soothing touch of a sister's hand, as he lay upon the pain-tossed couch of a hospital! Can we ever forget their sympathetic eyes, their low, soft-spoken words of encouragement and cheer when the result of the struggle between life and death yet hung in the balance. I am not a Catholic, but I stand ready at any and all times to defend these noble women, even with my life, for I owe that life to them.

These are the women, to paraphrase Father Leonard Feeney, who have no worldly ambitions, desire no fame, seek no romance, ask no reward offered on this earth; poor, chaste, obedient, anxious to be always the maximum of service to their Sisters and to their neighbors, and the minimum of annoyance; women with the loveliest manners existent in this world, modest, soft-voiced, invariably gay, to whom laughter comes as easily as sunlight; talking freely and easily because the practice of contemplation has taught them what it is valuable to speak, and holding more fondness for their parents in a single thought than all the married daughters do in a thousand; women feeling safest and most at home in their chapel where they will spend hours on end before the Blessed Sacrament, unmindful of any distress in back or knees; women beautiful in sickness and capable of bearing pain more silently than any creature of this earth; modest and undramatic in their death, asking only to be laid in the graveyard of their community as "one of the Sisters" and with a tombstone undistinguishable from any other, save for their name; vanishing out of this temporal scene with the expectation of a long Purgatory and insistent on having prayers said for them after death. If Father Tim had been gifted with the literary ability of a Feeney, these are the ideas he would have expressed in regard to the Sisters.

The Sisters of St. Joseph and later the Daughters of Charity of St. Vincent de Paul were his indispensable aids in running St. Patrick's school and the nursery. The Helpers of the Holy Souls visited families in the parish and reported their findings to the busy pastor. To the institutions of the Little Sisters of the Poor he committed many an aging man or woman. To the hospitals of various congregations, including the Sisters of St. Mary, the Daughters of Charity, and the Sisters of Mercy, he entrusted hundreds of sick and dying men and women during his long pastorate. And his own slim purse was always open to help their enterprises as far as possible.

His esteem for the guardians of law and order and for the Sisters was so genuine that they were willing to overlook his outbursts of temper, his occasional sharp criticisms, and his authoritative or even autocratic manner. Almost everybody felt that way about Father Tim. One could overlook the defects of a man who was always trying to find the good in somebody else. One could forgive a man who, like St. Paul, tried to make himself all things to all men.

Chapter 15

ALL THINGS TO ALL MEN

FROM some of the tributes paid to Father Tim, the impression might be gained that he had no faults and made no mistakes. A more searching study of his character and works reveals that such an impression is erroneous. Father Tim had his faults, made his mistakes. And he would have been the first to admit this.

Father Dempsey's weakness in regard to drink as a young priest had been overcome by a stiff regimen of prayer and self-denial. He himself did not go so far as to take the heroic pledge of total abstinence; but he had a wholesome respect for those who took such a pledge and he encouraged others to take it. He would say of a man: "He never took a drink in his life," or "He never broke his Confirmation pledge."

For women he ever retained the high ideals that years of prayer and study during his preparatory period had engraved imperishably on the tablet of his heart. He looked up and saw a woman of radiance, dressed in white and blue, and heard her startling words, "I am the Immaculate Conception." With the simplicity of a child he put his hand in her own white, loving hand and so walked through life with her. Temptations at times beat on the citadel of his soul, but the walls were too strong, the defenders too courageous: God and Father Tim were a majority.

As for money, the praiseworthy and legitimate desire to obtain what was needed for church, school, and charitable purposes never degenerated into a personal attachment to it, a grasping for it under any self-delusion. During his lifetime Father Dempsey handled hundreds of thousands of other people's dollars; yes, handled, not hoarded. He spent little on himself and his personal needs, little on his relatives. The hundreds of thousands were spent on his institutional works, on needy families and individuals. He had practical experience of the promise that poverty of spirit makes a person happy. This made him adamant against the seductive wiles of money.

But shortage of money, that made his gray hairs white, was a temptation in another way. In those dark days when he couldn't see how to put milk in the bottles and glasses of the youngsters at the nursery, how to provide clean linens for the beds in the Hotel for Men and the Hotel for Women, how to get coal in the coalbins of his institutions, he did a lot of worrying. Like oppressive gray clouds, moods of discouragement would come over him, to be dispelled at last by a providential donation that would carry the works along for a while. Even habitual trust in God as firm as the Rocky Mountains may not exclude occasional temporary worry in a man of acutely sensitive nature.

The mellowing of character that came gradually with the passage of the years and an ever widening experience of human nature tended to diminish the impetuosity that had marked Father Tim's early years at St. Patrick's. His flarings of impatience were less frequent, his apologies quicker. He could still speak strong language when anger stirred his soul. An energetic man, used to initiating important enterprises and carrying them through to a conclusion, could hardly be expected to play 'possum when he thought his rights or the rights of the people he lived for were being violated. He had a mind on persons and things, and he spoke that mind fearlessly, let the chips fall where they may. He was not the man to use weasel words.

A competent manager himself, he could scarcely bear with good humor the interference or even well-intentioned efforts at cooperation of people less competent than himself. Yet his method of getting his subordinates to do things was most gracious. He rarely issued a formal command. It was enough to say, "Would you mind doing this-and-that?" or "It would be nice if you would do this." Yet little initiative on the part of assistants was specifically encouraged by him, although in later years of his life he seemed to be willing to give up some of his control.

It is no easy thing to know another man's motives and intentions; they belong to that intangible realm of the spiritual where God and the soul and the good and bad spirits struggle to settle eternal issues. We may easily know what a person says and what a person does; we may not so easily know his reasons for it. That's why Christ warned against judging others.

The facts about Father Dempsey's institutional works and services to society can be ascertained. His Hotel for Men corrected the roving disposition of many men and led them to establish homes of their own; provided a decent temporary home with attractive surroundings; secured work through the Free Employment Bureau; protected the indigent against exorbitant interest; reformed lives and helped to keep others straight. It was his example which inspired men like Father E. J. Flanagan of Omaha, Father Peter Wynhoven of New Orleans, and others in half a dozen or more cities to open similar hotels. His hotel broke down prejudice against the Church, and made it easier for thousands of men to save their souls. In the course of thirty years he provided over 500,000 free lodgings and about 300,000 free meals at the Men's Hotel.

His Exiles' Rest gave burial to 220 people from 1909 to 1936. The Day Nursery and Emergency Home served to preserve or reunite hundreds of families, comforted working mothers by its services to their children, and introduced many children into the Christ-life, the life of grace. The Hotel for Women provided a good home at low cost or for nothing for working women and girls, a temporary home for women whose children were being taken care of in the nursery, protected working girls from dangers, and secured work in respectable families and firms through a Free Labor Agency. Women in temporary distress were helped; a wholesome environment was offered in which twenty-five religious vocations flowered; about 150,000 free lodgings, and 200,000 free meals were provided; and many women came into the Church.

His parole work was a strong factor in the rehabilitation of hundreds of prisoners. Detective Sergeant Thomas J. Moran, head of the Parole Bureau in St. Louis, said, "He could take a heavier load and do more with it than people like ourselves because the parolees had such confidence in him. Former inmates dislike social workers and visits to their homes. They came to Father Tim. He made an important contribution to the care of parolees, and was ahead of parole officers in this, that he had the men contact him between report periods."

His conciliation, mediation, and arbitration in connection with more than thirty major strikes prevented the loss of hundreds of lives, of hundreds of thousands of dollars worth of property, and of countless working hours, the long-continued existence of strained relations between employers and employees, and hardships of all kinds for the general public.

His efforts to pacify gangs, although not entirely successful, at least insured periods of tranquillity and safety in St. Louis during the 1920's. His White Cross Crusade gave employment to a hundred men and raised revenue for the support of the institutional works. The Convalescent Home provided a few thousand women with decent surroundings where they could regain their strength. His Free Lunch Room gave out 5,673,917 free lunches from November, 1931, to April, 1936, saved many a man from despair and suicide, and served as an outlet for the generosity of hundreds of firms and individuals in St. Louis. His short-lived Home for the Colored furnished about 100,000 free lodgings and proved to the colored the Church's maternal interest in their welfare.

These are some of the facts, but what about the motives? Could mere personal ambition, desire for praise, or humanitarian considerations have been the impelling force behind his thirty-eight years of unique pastoral work? An examination of Father Dempsey's own words and deeds, and of the judgments of others in regard to him, forces an impartial critic to rule out such less worthy motives. They don't have the power to bind a man to a grueling life of service to the poor and to the community for thirty-eight years in a poverty-stricken parish. To try to explain his long life of service by such motives would be like trying to explain the illumination of a whole city by one storage battery. The storage battery just hasn't got "the stuff."

Moreover, as a priest he would be entitled to the presumption that his motives were more worthy. A priest is dedicated to a supernatural way of life. He has freely chosen to follow Christ the hard way. He has answered the call to be a mediator between God and man, to do the works of Christ. This was the call that young Tim Dempsey responded to as a little lad in Ireland; this was the call to which he faithfully corresponded during long and sometimes tiresome and trying years of training; this was the call which he esteemed above all others from his early days. He tried to act always from a pure motive of the love of God and men.

Incidents narrated about Father Tim bring out the fact that he believed he was serving Christ when he helped a fellow man; that he looked upon men not as so many economic symbols or as guinea pigs for social experimentation or as mere physico-chemical machines but as made in their souls to the likeness of God, created, redeemed, and sanctified or to be sanctified by the Most Blessed Trinity. To him it was so much empty verbiage to prate about the brotherhood of men without the fatherhood of God, as the communists do. He had no sympathy for the secularized and naturalized *fraternité* introduced by eighteenth-century philosophy and propagated by the French Revolution and nineteenth-century liberalism. To Father Tim the central fact of the universe and of all times — the Incarnation of the Son of God — was an overwhelmingly important fact. That taking of flesh by the Son of God made Christ the Elder Brother of the human family. His faith was the basis of a charity that is sometimes confused with mere philanthropy.

To confuse Divine charity with a merely human philanthropy would be like confusing a dog's barking with President Roosevelt's Fireside Chats. The basis of philanthropy "is a purely human knowledge of the poor, gained only from scientific observation," according to Father Paul H. Furfey, "and the methods are the mere expedients of a modern scientific social work." On the other hand, the methods of true scientific social work, as properly taught and inspired by sound Christian sentiment, can be of the highest value and of the greatest possible helpfulness to the client.

"Philanthropy, in the exact sense of the word — love of man —," says Arnold Lunn, "is seldom found except in a religious setting, for it is one thing to work for the benefit of humanity, as many secularists have done, it is quite another matter to love men. Indeed, there would seem to be some necessary connection between the first and the second great commandments, for the saints aflame with love of God have found it easier than other people to love their neighbors."

The reformer inspired by the love of God, as Father Tim was, begins with the individual person and hopes to affect the social structure through the individual; the humanitarian begins with the social structure and hopes to affect the individual through the social environment. At least, with the humanitarian, the social structure occupies the first place. Father Dempsey did not disregard social environment and social structure, but he placed the emphasis on the individual person.

As Chesterton says of St. Francis of Assisi, Father Dempsey "did not see the mob for the men. What distinguishes this very genuine democrat from any mere demagogue is that he never either deceived or was deceived by the illusion of mass suggestion. Whatever his taste in monsters, he never saw before him a many-headed beast. He only saw the image of God multiplied but never monotonous. To him a man was always a man and did not disappear in a dense crowd any more than in a desert."

What gave to this American social apostle his extraordinary personal power was this: that from the highest ecclesiastic to the lowest down-and-outer, from the highest civil officer to the most wretched, bloated, bleary-eyed drunk, there was never a man who looked into those sparkling blue eyes without being certain that Tim Dempsey "was really interested in *him;* in his own inner individual life, from the cradle to the grave; that he himself was being valued and taken seriously, and not merely added to the spoils of some social policy or the names in some clerical document."

The impersonal, office-hour type of charitable service – which must never be confused with the Catholic idea of truly scientific social work – was as repugnant to Father Dempsey as the wearing of orange on St. Patrick's Day. His own method might best be described as personalist social reform, the characteristic technique of the early Church. This means the social effect of the practice of the social virtues by the individual person; it means social reform through personal reform. As Arnold Lunn says:

> The Catholic Church produces many saints like Father Claver, who have a vocation for the reform of individuals rather than of institutions, saints whose first instinct is to relieve immediate distress, and bind up the wounds of those in their immediate neighborhood while leaving to others the task of changing the institutions responsible for the evil which they deplore. Father Claver was so occupied with slaves that he had little time to think about slavery.

This personal interest springing from a true love for men flowered in a courteous hospitality. Like Francis of Assisi or St. John Vianney, the curate of Ars, Father Dempsey in the bare and barren simplicity of his life had clung to one rag of luxury: the manners of a court.

> But whereas in a court there is one king and a hundred courtiers, [says Chesterton] in this story there was one courtier moving among a hundred kings. For he treated the whole mob of men as a mob of kings. And this was really and truly the only attitude that will appeal to that part of man to which he wished to appeal. It cannot be done by giving gold or even bread; for it is a proverb that any reveler may fling largesse in mere scorn. It cannot even be done by giving time and attention; for any number of philanthropies and benevolent bureaucrats do such work with a scorn far more cold and horrible in their hearts. No plans or proposals or efficient rearrangement will give back to a broken man his self-respect and sense of speaking with an equal. One gesture will do it.

Father Tim's openhearted hospitality made St. Patrick's rectory the mecca of Catholics, Protestants, Jews, and nonsectarians, Democrats, Republicans, Socialists, senators, governors, mayors, labor leaders, employers, workers, millionaires, the very poor, and the middle class, actors, fighters, musicians, and people of all walks of life and from all parts of the world. By way of illustration we may mention John McCormack the singer, Sam Gompers of the A. F. of L., Ed Wynn and Katharine Hepburn of stage and screen, Jack Dempsey the heavyweight boxing champ, Msgr. Bonzano and Cardinal Vanutelli. Toward all his manners were simple and unaffected; he was above human respect. What the Protestant George Barrow said of Irish hospitality can well be applied to Father Tim: ". . . not all the authority of the Pope or the Cardinals could induce him to close his doors on Luther himself, were that respectable personage at present alive and in need of food and refuge. Honor to Ireland and her 'hundred thousand welcomes.' "

Although Father Tim was an expert in advising the thousands who came to him for guidance and help and although his disposition was naturally happy and his sense of humor highly developed, yet his own spiritual life did not always run smoothly. He was a scrupulous man; and, according to

Father Faber, "A scrupulous man teases God, irritates his neighbor, torments himself, and oppresses his director." Perhaps a partial explanation of Father Dempsey's ceaseless activity may be found in his struggle to beat the spiritual disease of scruples. Perhaps he was bothered with scruples because his high soul was climbing the high way with the excessive ardor of a naturally fervent disposition.

> To every man there openeth
> A Way, and Ways, and a Way.
> And the High Soul climbs the High Way,
> And the Low Soul gropes the Low,
> And in between, on the misty flats,
> The rest drift to and fro.

The low soul groping the low way and the rest drifting to and fro on the misty flats are scarcely ruffled by such a thing as scruples.

A long siege of this disease may have the effect of utterly discouraging a man, literally unmanning him, rendering him unfit for daily struggle, a coward in the face of danger. But in Father Tim's case it seems that the gift of fortitude won out. It was the courage of a dauntless soldier of Christ that led him to establish his many works and manage them successfully through the long years.

It was the courage of a St. Philip Neri that led him to spend his long life among the masses in the St. Patrick's district in St. Louis. He revealed his strength of will in struggling against debt, in eliminating non-Catholic mission groups which tried to lure children away from St. Patrick's, in bearing patiently the attacks of lying and calumniating tongues, and in withstanding the envy and jealousy of certain individuals. It took courage to engage in the corporal and spiritual works of mercy and to live the Beatitudes. It took courage to remain faithful to that high ideal of striving to model his life after Him who is the Way, the Truth, and the Life, after Him who is Love Incarnate.

This was the active Father Tim, the man of busy full days

in the service of the poor and of the whole community. This was the aggressive Father Tim who could recover from a long and dangerous siege of bronchial pneumonia in 1934 and predict with a smile, "I'll live to be 125, as did St. Patrick," the Father Tim who, despite his high blood pressure, could boast in the summer of 1935, "I'm feeling in better health today than I was 37 years ago when I first became pastor of St. Patrick's."

ST. LOUIS POST-DISPATCH,

FATHER TIM.

This is the text of Father Tim's life: "Come unto me, all ye that labor and are heavy laden, and I will give you rest." Perhaps he would not like to have it put so solemnly, for it was his manner to succor the unfortunate with charming Irish gaiety. He turned away effusiveness with a witty phrase, a pat on the back, a refreshing smile. He liked to provide warm soup for empty stomachs and clean beds for tired bodies, and no man or woman appealed to him in vain. In him, the "sweet milk of human kindness" flowed.

It was not one of Father Tim's least achievements that the example of his own broad sympathies induced a sympathy in others. His work among the poor and lowly attracted the interest of the rich and powerful. As the scope of the priest's charities widened, so did his financial necessities, but the money was always forthcoming in generous measure. And it was given warmly and graciously by men and women who, by that token, felt they were privileged to share in the masterpiece that was Father Tim's life.

It was a countryman of Father Tim's, John Boyle O'Reilly, the Irish poet, who wrote the searing lines:

The organized charity, scrimped and iced,
In the name of a cautious, statistical Christ.

Father Tim's soup lines, his hotels for working men and women, his day nursery and convalescent home, and all the rest of his varied activities, furnished the complete antithesis. Here was charity that sprang from Father Tim's deep love for his fellow man, a love that asked no questions, plied no creed, but gave fully and freely.

Farewell to a great human being!

Chapter 16

IT COMES TO EVERY MAN

PREMONITIONS of the end that comes to every man were not taken seriously by Father Tim despite his dangerous condition of high blood pressure. He continued as before to make good the statement once uttered concerning him by Rabbi Leon Harrison: "There is no citizen more useful in St. Louis."

Largely through Father Tim's untiring efforts a long and violent strike by the Gas House Workers' Union at the Laclede Gas Light Company, March to July, 1935, was finally settled. Not without the best of reasons the executive board of the Central Trades and Labor Union adopted a resolution calling him "one of God's noblemen by every test, by every word and kindly deed, and the friend of every race and creed." Even now, an arbitration board, appointed by Mayor Bernard F. Dickmann to handle the dispute between the colored and the white motion-picture operators in August, 1935, was headed by Father Dempsey.

Nor did his bad physical condition prevent him from keeping up with essential correspondence. He had always loved to write to priests and other friends in many parts of the world, debating with them issues of the day and exchanging pleasantries. In February, 1936, he wrote to his old friend, former Senator Harry B. Hawes, in Washington, D. C.:

My Dearest Friend:

I was talking to your brother Richard, and he told me you were not so well, and you know how I felt. It will soon be forty years (1896) since we first met at the Fair Grounds. I never forget anything in my life, men's names, women's names, telephone numbers, etc.

Without *you* I would not have any place for the poor.

Thirty years ago you brought me to see John F. Lee, Bert Walker, Gussie Busch. I was very poor, had many financial entanglements, but "you plucked my feet from the net."

Since that fine day I have been able to weather every storm.

There is compensation in every condition of life. When I had nothing, I was in perfect health. When I got on my feet, and had financial difficulties removed, I got sick — that is, *blood pressure* gripped me. Apart from this, I never had a headache, toothache or any pain. Now I feel real well. For years I cannot take any kind of drink. I live very simply.

Now I must be *personal.* I do not know how you are financially. If you need anything that I have, tell me and it will be yours.

As ever

Devotedly,

(Signed) FATHER TIM

P.S. I am sending a medal of St. Patrick and St. Bridget. Wear it. It is blessed. Love to the Mrs. and Peyton and Eppes and Colonel. T.D.

When Father Tim called on the archbishop in April, 1936, he could still say that, despite high blood pressure, he was feeling "real well." The archbishop remarked, "You look florid; how do you feel?" "Fit as a fiddle," said Father Tim. He had been working hard on a serious strike involving two thousand union workers on twenty-two WPA projects in St. Louis city and county and had brought the strike to a conclusion only two days before, that is, on April 2.

At five o'clock Palm Sunday morning, April 5, 1936, he rose from bed with his customary "Glory be to God" on his lips. After saying the six o'clock Mass he breakfasted with his sister, Mary Kate, who during her thirty-six years as housekeeper had become as much like her brother as a woman possibly could. As they partook of orange juice, toast, bacon and eggs, he was his usual humorous and cheerful self. Before the 8, 9:30, and 11 o'clock Masses he greeted his parishioners at the entrance of old St. Patrick's and ushered them to their pews. Sometime in the morning he went to confession.

At noon he welcomed several labor union leaders at the rectory. They talked over plans for remodeling the parish school and renovating the somewhat dark and dingy old rectory. What a difference a coat of stucco, new tiling, and modification of the cupola had made in the church. In appreciation of Father Dempsey's long years of service as a conciliator, companies and unions had just recently transformed, free of charge, the red brick church into an attractive Spanish mission structure. The transformation would have cost $12,000. The *Star-Times* commented: "Union plasterers, lathers, slate and tile workers and union building laborers working without pay suggest that if Monsignor Dempsey's philosophy of life were more generally applied, the scarred exterior of the edifice of modern civilization might also take on a more attractive look."

After finishing his business with the labor leaders, he spent a few minutes with his 186 lodgers at the Men's Hotel. Later Mother St. Andrew of the Helpers of the Holy Souls came to consult him about her class for Negro children in the parish. After this two Jesuit Fathers and a Jesuit seminarian and some laymen arrived to prepare men for confession. As usual Father Tim regaled them with stories.

After Benediction his chauffeur drove him to the home of his sisters, Sarah and Agnes, in Webster Groves. Only in the past year or so had he submitted to riding in an automobile. While he was in good health, he always walked or took a streetcar for his necessary traveling. He used to say, "I don't want an auto. The streetcars are good enough for my boys, for my poor people; and that holds for me." He had to have a chauffeur to drive the donated auto because he was too nervous to drive. Because of the poor condition of his health he had been lately advised by his doctor to spend a few nights each week at the suburban home of his sisters where he would not be bothered by telephone calls and visitors.

A scrupulous man, Father Tim stopped on the way to go

to confession again, the second time that day. From the church he telephoned his sisters so they wouldn't worry about him being a bit late. After a pleasant evening conversing and listening to the radio, he retired at nine o'clock. At one in the morning, April 6, his sister Agnes was roused from slumber by a firm tapping on her door. It was Father Tim.

"Gath," he said, using her pet name, "I'm not so good. I think the wheezing in my chest is coming back."

His other sister, Sash or Sarah, called to him to put on his slippers. "Don't worry, Sash. I've got 'em on."

He shuffled back to his room and settled himself in his big black leather-covered chair. His face seemed drained of color. His eyes were as lusterless as the reverse side of a tapestry. The lines on either side of his lips were like furrows. His chin rested on his chest. He looked bad. Sarah suggested that a priest and a doctor be called. He nodded feeble assent.

The Rev. Walter Tucker of the Church of the Holy Redeemer gave the last Sacraments to fortify him for the death struggle, "*Proficiscere anima Christiana*" . . . "Set out, O Christian soul." The doctor, David M. Skilling, Jr., after a hasty examination, nodded to the priest to proceed quickly. Once Father Tim smiled. Then he murmured the name of his sister, "Agnes." The two sisters thought they heard him say with his last breath, "Jesus, Mary." His eyes closed. Death had come about two o'clock.

Early in the morning his sister, Mary Kate, was told. Vincent and Frank were likewise shocked by the blow for a while. Interviewed by a reporter, Mary Kate remarked, "He seldom spoke of the future. He seemed to think he would live forever. . . . The men were in the soup line when they were told. I saw big men – men as big as Father Tim – break down and cry."

Monday, Tuesday, and Wednesday of Holy Week were days of mourning not only in the institutions and in the homes of the parish but in the whole city and for individuals in various parts of the country. The soft-spoken, humble, gray-haired day clerk at the hotel, Mr. Thomas Kelly, who had just relieved the ordinarily vivacious night clerk, Mr. Patrick McDonnell, said, "There's no skylarking in the halls, and no loud talking. These men have lost their best friend."

Each of the three large St. Louis daily papers, the *Globe-Democrat,* the *Post-Dispatch,* and the *Star-Times,* carried front page articles on Monday and devoted other parts of their pages to pictures and stories. For three days or more, facts about Father Tim – and some fiction – took precedence over legal squabbles, storms, political news, murders, and exhibition baseball games. A whole city paused to honor the memory of a well-beloved friend.

In the words of the *Star-Times* article for Monday:

> Father Tim is gone.
>
> In the church which he served forty-five years he bore the title of the Right Reverend Monsignor Timothy Dempsey, pastor of St. Patrick's at Sixth and Biddle streets.
>
> But to Catholics and Protestants and Jews of St. Louis, to the hungry and homeless and weary to whom he gave food and shelter and solace, to the gangsters whose bloody wars he helped to end, to hoboes from coast to coast, to the rich and the great of city and state and nation, to thieves and drunkards, to quarreling workers and employers whom he helped toward understanding — to all these he was just Father Tim, beloved beyond the measure of most men.

A reporter who wandered into the recreation room of the Men's Hotel in search of a story was stopped by an old man in a torn blue suit and dirty gray cap. "I hear you're down here to talk to us about Father Tim. Well, you see these friends of mine here" – and he swept his thin hand in the direction of the men sitting in the room – "we're just a 'problem' to some people, young people especially. But to Father Tim we were an opportunity. He looked at us and talked to us in a manner that showed he felt that way. He loved us.

"Some of us have seen people on the streets turn their glances from us as we passed. You've never experienced that and you wouldn't understand. When you are young, the world seems young, and when you are old, the world is old – and cold.

"But when Father Dempsey smiled and put out his hand – well, there was one warm and friendly spot in the world anyway. But I guess you don't quite understand." The old man scanned the reporter from head to foot. "You are still young."

That night hundreds of men, women, and children of many religious creeds and of no creed, of all stations in life, of all degrees of wealth and poverty, of almost all nationalities gazed upon the lifeless features of their priestly friend. The body had been prepared for burial at the Bensiek-Niehaus funeral parlors directly across the street from the church.

Catholic, Protestant, and Jewish clergymen, city officials, lawyers, doctors, and other professional men, business and industrial leaders, politicians, trade union men, gamblers, former bootleggers, policemen, firemen, common day-laborers, ragged beggars, women, and children, representing a cross-section of the life of the city, streamed democratically past the casket. Even in death Father Tim was reconciling the disparate elements of human society, harmonizing the discordant, and forcing upon men the realization of the truth that they were unified in the possession of a common humanity and in their obligations toward a fatherly God.

After the short evening services conducted by Father W. H. Reeves, Father M. F. Phelan, and Father J. P. Brennan, weeping men and sobbing women made their way up the aisle. An occasional high-pitched moan was heard. It seemed as if everyone who was anyone in St. Louis was there, and almost everyone who was no one. In fact, there were more of *these*. Two of the "no ones," poorly dressed and a bit unkempt, were standing in front of the church, debating whether to go in to have a look at Father Tim. One of them started in; the other drew back, objecting that his clothes were too ragged. "Come on," insisted his partner, tugging at his frayed sleeve, "why, Father Tim wouldn't know you if you were all dressed up." They entered to pay their respects. All night long people continued to come. Night workers stopped on their way from work; people on the early shift stopped to pray before work.

Tuesday witnessed an almost continuous flow of people to St. Patrick's. Department stores, factories, and offices seemed to have emptied their workers into the church for a last look at their friend. A group of little colored children entered in the afternoon and boldly approached the usher. "Mistah," said their spokesman, his round eyes pleading, "will you all lift each of us up so we kin see Faddah Tim?" Later a poor old colored man, clad in rags and weeping bitterly and unashamedly, approached the bier. The old Negro looked on the face of the dead priest, turned his tear-dimmed eyes toward the altar, fell upon his knees, and cried out from the depths of his soul, "Lawd, have mercy on him." That night diocesan and regular clergy under the leadership of the Most Rev. Christian H. Winkelmann chanted the solemn Office of the Dead.

One old unlettered man gave expression to his sincere sentiments in a penciled note which he handed to the Rev. George Hamilton, S.J., an instructor at St. Patrick's. The handwriting is poor, words are misspelled, capitalization is incorrect, punctuation is almost lacking, the paper is poor, the grammar is defective, yet it's a great human document.

> to whom it may Concern I am writing this note to tell you that i have known father Tim Demcy since he was two years and have always known him to be one of the most godly men and haveknown him to be a good Charrityable man and most loving to all men and women and to Children. Especaly 2 years ago father Called me in his house and asked were I was staying and i told him truth. I told him that I was staying in an old stable like our Dear Savour was Born in. I told him I never thought that i was better than hour Savour was. and father told me to go to his hotel for ever and ever.

At seven o'clock Wednesday morning, three hours before the time for the funeral Mass, people began to assemble outside the church. By ten o'clock nearly 5000 men, women, and children, Catholic and non-Catholic, black and white, of all ages and conditions of life, stood along Sixth Street and Biddle Street in the bright morning sun. Over 700 clergymen, Sisters, and laymen were inside. A hush settled over the vast crowd as Archbishop Glennon, assisted by Msgr. Dunne as archpriest, by Father J. J. Lonergan as deacon, and by Father P. J. O'Connor as subdeacon, began with the "*In nomine Patris, et Filii, et Spiritus Sancti*" at the foot of the altar. Father D. J. Lavery and Father J. J. Butler were deacons of honor, and Father Alfred Thomson and Father C. H. Helmsing were master of ceremonies and assistant master respectively.

After the Gospel the sacrifice was halted in its sacred, dramatic action for the sermon. All eyes were on Monsignor Crane, the vicar-general. Almost breathless, the congregation listened to his reading of St. Matthew's account of the Last Judgment which emphasizes the corporal works of mercy. Then said the speaker simply, "You will find the sermon already preached. It is the life of Father Dempsey." For nearly a half hour he offered an interpretation of that life.

"Father Dempsey's life was a life of continued service," he said emphatically, surveying the throng which included a great number of clergy, representatives of the various sisterhoods, the mayor and his aides, hundreds of men from the labor unions and employers' associations, and others whose lives had in some intimate way touched the life of Father Tim. "It was a life lived for others. It was like the life of our Blessed Lord.

"The motive of Father Dempsey's life was the seeking of souls. This has been the cry of the saints through the ages, 'Give me souls!' Behind the twinkle and the smile and the pleasing remarks and the humor of Father Dempsey there was always that which was fundamental in his life, the knowledge of the value of souls. . . . Behind the poorest specimen of humanity, behind the shriveled face of the worst man or woman who ever came to him, he saw the soul for which the Son of God died. He saw through the flesh to the soul."

The congregation stirred a bit as the Monsignor touched on Father Tim's methods. "To the poor he was always kind, merciful, and sympathetic. Father Dempsey was not a modernist in his social activities. He had no 'file'; he had no 'case records.' He saw no man or woman as 'Number 72,' but as a sufferer who had dignity, even though in poverty. No king or queen ever has any more majesty before God than the poor suffering man or woman in low estate. He realized completely the doctrine of the Mystical Body of Christ: if one suffer, then the whole body suffers, because you are one in Christ."

The two hundred and fifty men from the Central Trades and Labor Union, the Building Trades Council, and individual unions and the representatives of the employing groups followed with special interest his treatment of the next topic. "His activity in labor organizations caused thousands to recognize his worth. The Catholic manifesto of the rights of man is the letter of Pope Leo XIII on the Condition of Labor. Father Dempsey was not merely a theoretical student of that doctrine. He lived it out, on the principle of justice. There can be no social security unless it be built around justice. Men will be dissatisfied, men will be unhappy until they feel justice is rendered. The different organizations are here, attesting their gratitude for what Father Dempsey has done for them through the years. The music which you heard outside before the Mass was the tribute of his loving friends of the Musicians' Union."

A few nervous coughs and clearing of throats preceded Monsignor Crane's climax. "Our Lord said, 'I am the resurrection and the life. He that believeth in Me, though he were dead, yet shall he live.' This was the faith in which Father Dempsey lived and in which he died. His life was for the poor and the unfortunate, and I suppose for that reason he died, because he did not know what rest was. There is no case file left in Father Dempsey's papers. There are no records of investigations. But we shall find that He who knows all things kept a record in the Book of Life."

During the after-sermon pause and usual coughing and stirring, the imaginations of many must have pictured the eulogized Father Tim in the sanctuary delivering sermons with simplicity, directness, clearness, and force. With sadness they realized that now those lips were sealed, that tongue was stilled, that melodious voice was mute. They would have to wait now until resurrection day.

After the absolution of the corpse at the end of Mass the active pallbearers, Messrs. Daniel Murphy, James Burke, Timothy Cronin, L. H. Schulte, William Ryan, and William Maul, chosen by Father Tim himself from the Teamsters' and Chauffeurs' Union, took their places near the heavy casket. As the procession emerged from the church and moved south on Sixth Street, the thousands of curious and sorrowing spectators watched with bared heads and serious faces. Many heads could be seen at the windows of near-by shops and plants; some people secured positions of vantage on the roofs. Mounted police ranged up and down the street to keep a passage open. The band from the Musicians' Union gave expression to the emotions of the crowd by its solemn and touching playing of Chopin's Funeral March. The old bell in St. Patrick's tower, whose metallic voice had called the people to worship during the long years of Father Tim's pastorate, at sad-hearted Danny Buckley's pull sounded a solemn and heavy "good-by" to Father Tim.

Along the funeral route to Calvary, Jewish merchants stood in white-aproned reverence before their fish markets and grocery stores. Uniformed policemen and firemen stood at attention to honor the memory of their beloved friend, the man who called the police "the most charitable people in the world" and knew most of the firemen by their first names. Old men and women, boys and girls, blacks and whites, paused to pay their respects. At the entrance to Calvary, where a sizeable stone crucifix speaks a message of hope and victory, the drivers had to pick their way cautiously through the throng. It took the cortege of over 300 cars a half hour to pass a specified point. Among the hundreds of automobiles were 25 taxicabs, donated for the occasion by Ed Hardy and Frank Foley of the Black and White Taxicab Company out of respect for their dead friend and for the convenience of old and infirm persons.

Under the canvas canopy at "The Exiles' Rest" Msgr. Crane gave the Church's final blessing. Father Tim's brothers and sisters watched with broken hearts the lowering of the casket into the hallowed ground. The simple ceremony was over as the two buglers, one near, the other at a distance, sounded taps and the response. There the mortal remains of Father Tim were to await the Resurrection, surrounded by his more than two hundred poor friends under the shadow of the Celtic Cross, those friends of whom he had said, "I just put them all together so they'd all get up in a bunch and maybe say a good word for me when the trumpet blows."

That very day Representative John J. Cochran of Missouri gave a brief speech on Father Tim from the floor of the National House of Representatives at Washington for inclusion in the Congressional Record. At the request of the *Globe-Democrat* Harry Hawes gave public expression to his feelings about the dead priest.

"Fun and humanity and fine common sense were his strong points.

"While Father Tim leaned a bit over the Democratic side politically (as most of his constituents were Democrats), that made no difference with the Republican officials and politicians. They liked him, respected him, and helped him. . . .

"There is no one to take his place — no one has the smile or heart of big Father Tim. None of us ever thought of calling him Monsignor. He would not have liked it, and we always tried to do the thing that Father Tim liked.

"One day I asked him how he was getting along feeding his

boarders when food was so high. He said it worried him a great deal, and he even had under consideration a plan to charge them 'a nickel a week more.'

"That was Father Tim."

The readers of the St. Louis newspapers were interested in the Archbishop's tribute to Father Tim.

"Father Dempsey died because his heart was too big," said the venerable Archbishop to reporters. "All his emotions were centered in his heart. He was a unique personality – one of the kind which can have no successor. He was intensely charitable, but with it all always kept the Irish element in his heart; that is to say, he was bright, witty, a good student, and he had a flair for the poetic.

"His death will be a great loss to the community. I feel keenly the loss of Monsignor Dempsey. The poor who have been his wards for so many years, who have been his first care, have lost a faithful friend. Everybody liked Tim Dempsey."

The day after the funeral Msgr. Crane, Vincent Dempsey, and attorney Harry G. Whelan filed Father Tim's will in Probate Court, with Edward Wunnenberg and Joe Carlavato as witnesses. "The value of the whole estate," said Vincent, "is $9,064. Father Tim spent $40,000 for the purchase of real estate and as much or more in enlarging and improving the buildings used for his Charities. I estimate the cost of operating all the Charities at $5000 a month."

The will, dated November 4, 1935, read in part: "Whatever assets I have, I have received for distribution to the poor, which I have done so far as I could; and whatever remains after my death may be so distributed." A thousand dollars was left to Msgr. Crane for Masses for Father Tim's intentions; the remainder of the estate was to be equally divided between the Little Sisters of the Poor, a sisterhood devoted to the care of old people, and the Helpers of the Holy Souls, a sisterhood devoted to caring for the poor and sick in parishes.

Tributes to the dead priest continued to pour in. The Rt.

Rev. William Scarlett, Bishop of the Episcopal Diocese of Missouri, styled Father Tim "a man who cannot easily be spared . . . an unusual man, so kindly, possessing such deep sympathies and broad views, and a wonderful record of notable service. He exerted a profound influence in this community, and he himself was a warm bond uniting various groups."

Rabbi Ferdinand M. Isserman of Temple Israel, St. Louis, stated that "Because of his genuine consecration to the underprivileged, to the friendless in the city, many of the members of my congregation had a genuine appreciation and affection for him and stood behind him in many of his public activities."

A life-long friend of Father Dempsey, Senator Bennett C. Clark of Missouri, who keeps a colored picture of the priest on the wall of his senate office in Washington, esteemed Father Tim as "the most useful citizen of the city of St. Louis, barring nobody. He was also one of the grandest men and one of the sweetest characters that it has ever been my privilege to know, or know about. To know him was to love him. It was a privilege to me to assist him in a humble way in the wonderful work which he did so many years in our community. It was a priceless privilege to have enjoyed his intimate personal friendship. No man in my acquaintance in the city of St. Louis has been more universally mourned in his passing than Father Tim."

The Central Trades and Labor Union of St. Louis unanimously adopted a resolution that said, among other things, "His passing deprives St. Louis of one of her greatest, most useful citizens . . . we shall always remember the altruistic, sympathetic, charitable spirit which characterized his life as a lofty example of sterling citizenship – of a life well lived." The late Mr. William M. Brandt, secretary, called him "one of the grandest characters that ever lived. He was a true friend of the working people, who have suffered a great loss in his death." The secretary of the Building Trades Council prophesied, "His memory will be an inspiration to all who knew him to carry on to better things in his name."

The sports editor of the *Globe-Democrat,* Mr. Maurice O. Shevlin, took the sportsman's slant. "Father Tim is gone – and the hearts of St. Louis soccer fans are heavy. They mourn the passing of their stanchest friend, the benevolent Irish priest whose sincere interest in their sport was no less than his love for mankind . . . this year he contributed one of the finest, perhaps the finest, soccer teams in the nation, the Shamrocks, three times national champions, who only Sunday, a few hours before their patron's death, won their way into the final round of the annual national championship play with a victory in Pittsburgh."

The Board of Directors of the St. Louis Convention, Publicity, and Tourist Bureau was impressed by "the many lessons of the brotherhood of men. . . . Father Tim's life stands out as an exemplification of all those lessons. In him, the good Samaritan lives again. . . . Faith, hope, and charity have made him rich beyond all earthly values."

The local religious and secular newspapers and magazines as well as papers in various parts of the nation published articles on Father Tim and editorialized on his life. On April 14 the papers carried the news that the Rev. James P. Johnston, pastor of St. Malachy's church, had been appointed to the difficult position of pastor of St. Patrick's and manager of the Father Dempsey Charities. To stimulate interest in the Charities and to keep the memory of Father Dempsey alive and fresh, a memorial service, attended by a thousand people and honored by a telegram from the president of the United States, was held on June 7 in Convention Hall at the Municipal Auditorium.

In a brief talk at this memorial service the Archbishop stressed Father Tim's dedication to the poor. "More than once I offered Father Dempsey a new St. Patrick's where he would be relieved of the arduous tasks he had set himself to do; in the country, where the air was fresh and the trees green. . . .

In his mind there was no laboring class, no capitalist class. There was only one great human brotherhood. He lived with the poor he loved; he did not despise riches. He merely thought that those who were rich should help those who were poor. In the democracy of the dead of Exiles' Rest he lies asleep. Born poor, he lived poor and died poor. His monument is in the hearts of the living."

A memorial brochure, entitled *Right Reverend Monsignor Timothy Dempsey — His Life and Charities,* was published by the Burgess Printing Company in the fall of 1936. Father Tim had asked that nothing distinctive should mark his grave among the poor in The Exiles' Rest, but the Archbishop arranged to have a granite memorial slab laid over the grave in May, 1937. At the solemn blessing of this memorial on May 30 he said to the five-hundred gathered at The Exiles' Rest:

"Father Dempsey, the exile, did contribute his part to the life-stream of America, casting on its surface a million flowers of charity, fixing in its depths the glorious heights of a divine faith, and illuminating it by the fervor of a priestly life." After the blessing he stopped at the grave of Mr. Isaac Gradwohl, a converted Jew who had been "one of Father Tim's first lieutenants in charity."

Father Tim had been devoted to Matt Talbot, the penitential Irish lumberman who said that "the kingdom of heaven was promised not to the sensible and the educated but to such as have the spirit of little children." He had insisted during the remodeling of the church that a niche be left in the wall that connected the church with the rectory. He had intended to put "somebody" in that niche, namely a statue of the saintly Dublin laborer, and had even engaged the services of a statuary firm. But Matt Talbot was not in that niche when Father Tim died.

Certain friends thought it would be better to have a bust of Father Dempsey himself in the niche instead of a statue of Matt Talbot. They engaged a sculptor, Mr. Charles A. Beaty. On October 30, 1938, the Feast of Christ the King, after the last Mass before a crowd estimated at three to four thousand the bust of Father Tim was unveiled in an impressive ceremony. It was dedicated by Archbishop Glennon on St. Patrick's day, March 17, 1939. At the base of the bust was the simple inscription:

"Father Tim: 1867–1936: A Man of God."

The magnificent influence of Father Tim had been exercised in his humble capacity as pastor of St. Patrick's. Yet that influence was widespread and no man can tell what its ultimate limits in the Providence of God will be.

As one might well say that the history of France between 1799 and 1815 is largely the history of Napoleon, so one may say that the history of St. Patrick's between 1896 and 1936 is largely the biography of Father Tim Dempsey. The parallel stops here, however, for Napoleon spent his days chiefly in a destructive type of war and died an outcast from civilized society on the bleak island of St. Helena off the coast of Africa, whereas Father Tim spent his long life in constructive work for men and died a hero and well-beloved by people in various parts of the world.

Catholics learned to love their Faith more because of his words and example. Non-Catholics who may have been suspicious of the Catholic Church or openly hostile learned to admire its principles and teachings as concretized and externalized in his life.

That he showed reasonable private toleration to people of various faiths is proved by the fact that Protestants of all kinds, Jews, and nonsectarians considered him their best friend. Many became Catholics through admiration for him and consequent curiosity about the Church which could produce a man of such universal sympathies, keen understanding of everybody's problems, and willingness to cooperate for the common good. We need but cite, in this connection, the case of Seneca Taylor, an important figure in St. Louis sport circles. But, like him, there were the hundreds of thousands of men, women, and children who in some way or other came under his beneficent influence as personally interested manager of the various charitable institutions and works.

Myles Connolly, in his famous character, Mr. Blue, has exquisitely summarized what one might well apply to describe the charm and influence of Father Tim:

"It is impossible to be with him an hour without breathing a new wholesome air, charged with beauty. It is impossible to be with him and not catch the spectacular glory of the present moment. At the power of his presence, before the eloquence of his eyes, poverty, neglect, and such trifles become as nothing. One feels bathed in a brilliant and even tangible light, for it is the light he sees, and which, he would have us believe, is about us on our gallant journey toward death. All the scales of pettiness fall off the soul. The spirit stands up, clean, shining, valiant, in an unconscious effort to match his.

"But then he is gone, with his tears and laughter and his dazzling glory. 'Come, come,' his eyes say. 'Behold the perilous road!' No one follows, I believe. And sometimes I wonder if he cares. 'You will die, stifled with comfortability and normality, choked by small joys and small sorrows.' Such is his warning as he goes. What can a man do with a fellow like that?"

Father Tim is gone, but not forgotten. He achieved an immortality, not only with God, but with men. He lost his life in order to find it. And those who never knew him personally, who never basked in the light of his beaming face, nor caught the merry twinkle in his eye, nor reveled in the bubbling spring of his kindly humor, nor felt the exaltation of his generous spirit of helpfulness, have missed one of the most inspiring and delightful experiences that can come to a human being.

IMPORTANT DATES AND EVENTS

October 21, 1867 – Birth at Cadamstown, Offaly (King's) County, Ireland.
August 29, 1881 – Studies at St. Mary's Seminary, Mullingar.
Date uncertain – Studies at diocesan seminary of Meath, Navan.
February 5, 1885 – Studies at St. Patrick's Foreign Missionary College, Carlow.
June 14, 1891 – Ordination to priesthood at Carlow, Ireland.
September 19, 1891 – Arrival in St. Louis, Mo., U. S. A.
September – Appointment as substitute pastor, Indian Creek, Monroe County, Mo.
November – St. Patrick's parish near Moberly, Mo. (?)
December, 1891 – Assistant pastor, St. John the Baptist, Moberly.
1893 – Assistant pastor, Holy Angels, St. Louis, Missouri.
1895 – Assistant pastor, Assumption, St. Louis, Mo.
March, 1898 – Acting pastor of St. Patrick's, St. Louis.
July 11, 1898 – Official appointment as pastor of St. Patrick's.
1899 – Inauguration of free parish school.
1904 – Louisiana Purchase Exposition in St. Louis.
December 22, 1906 – Formal opening, Hotel for Workingmen.
1908 – Laying of cornerstone of new cathedral in St. Louis.
June, 1908 – Member of committee to raise $500,000 for cathedral.
September, 1908 – Beginning of the Hotel Magazine.
About 1909 – Free Labor Agency at Hotel for Men.
Spring, 1909 – The Exiles' Rest in Calvary Cemetery.
1909 – City Centennial Week, St. Louis.

December 20, 1909 – 25th anniversary of Archbishop Glennon's ordination to the priesthood.

April, 1910 – Talk on Church and Labor at Goller Hall.

July, 1910 – Trip to Ireland.

December 7, 1910 – Formal opening of Nursery and Emergency Home.

July 24, 1911 – Formal opening of the Hotel for Women.

1911 – Member of the board of directors of the Aid Society for Inmates of State Penal and Reformatory Institutions.

October 12, 1913 – Formal opening of new Nursery.

August, 1915 – Beginning of career of strike settlements.

April 27, 1916 – Dedication of Kenrick Seminary.

June, 1916 – Silver Jubilee of ordination to priesthood.

1916 – Visit by papal delegate, Monsignor Bonzano.

1918 – Change of location of the Hotel for Women.

1921 ff. – Intervention in gang wars.

1922 – The White Cross Crusade.

March 17, 1923 – Silver Jubilee as pastor of St. Patrick's.

May 10, 1923 – Investiture as Right Reverend Monsignor.

November, 1924 – Addition of Convalescent Home to Hotel for Women.

1926 – Consecration of the new St. Louis cathedral.

1927 – Sicilian gangs.

1928 – 25th anniversary of Archbishop's arrival in St. Louis.

June, 1931 – Fortieth anniversary of ordination.

November 16, 1931 – The Free Lunchroom.

February, 1932 – The Home for the colored.

September, 1933–February, 1934 – Continuous mission.

December 20, 1934 – 50th anniversary of Archbishop's ordination.

1935 – Irish Pipers and Fife, Drum, and Bugle Corps.

April 6, 1936 – *The Death of Father Tim.*

April 8, 1936 – Burial in The Exiles' Rest in Calvary Cemetery.

April 13, 1936 – Successor, the Rev. James Johnston.

June 7, 1936 – Memorial service, convention hall in auditorium.

Fall, 1936 – Memorial brochure.
May 30, 1937 – Blessing of memorial slab at the grave.
October 30, 1938 – Unveiling of Dempsey's bust at St. Patrick's.
March 17, 1939 – Formal dedication of the bust.

THE DEMPSEY GENEALOGY

"The Dempseys are descended from Milesius, King of Spain, through the Heremon line. The ancient name was O'Dinasaigh and signifies 'Estimable.' The founder of the family was Rossa Failge, son of Cathire More, or Cathire the Great, King of Ireland, A.D. 144. The Dempseys are of the same descent as the O'Conors Faily. They were Princes and Lords of Clanmaliere and Offaly and were sometimes styled Barons of Phillipstown and Viscounts of Clanmaliere.

"Their territory of Clanmaliere embraced parts of the baronies of Geashill and Phillipstown, in Kings County, with part of Portnehinch, in Queens County, and part of Offaly, in Kildaire, including Monasterevan and the adjoining districts. . . .

"In the twelfth century they waged war against the Anglo-Normans under Strongbow, Earl of Pembroke, who, in the year 1173, together with his son-in-law, Robert de Quincy, or de Quincy, constable and standard-bearer of Leinster, marched at the head of a powerful force into Kildare and Offaly. The English were defeated with great slaughter by the Irish clans, commanded by the O'Dempseys, Chiefs of Clanmaliere, the standard-bearer, de Quincy, being among the slain.

"It was not until after the Elizabethan wars that the O'Dempsey's lost their possessions."

(Rooney, John, *A Genealogical History of Irish Families*, N. Y., O'Hart Pub. Co., No date, p. 334).

The Dempsey crest has a shield with a lion in the middle and with a sword at either corner above the lion. On top or over the shield stands another lion holding a sword. The field on the shield is red; the lion on the shield, in the middle, is white; the other is red. *Elatum a Deo non deprimat* is the reading.